Alexander Cowan

3 Hollies Close

Thurlaston

Le9 7tu

USBORNE SCIENCE & EXPERIMENTS

ENERGY & POWER

Richard Spurgeon and Mike Flood

Edited by Corinne Stockley

Designed by Stephen Wright

Illustrated by Kuo Kang Chen and Joseph McEwan

Additional designs by Christopher Gillingwater

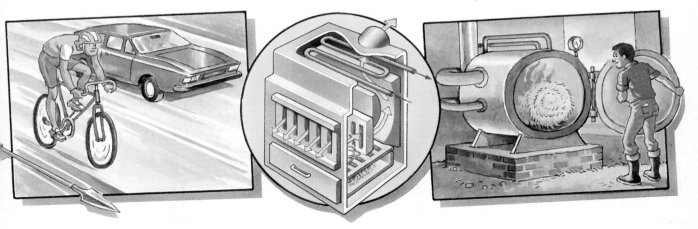

Contents

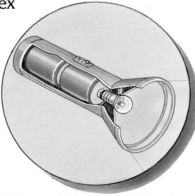

First published in 1990 by Usborne Publishing Ltd, 20 Garrick Street, London WC2E 9BJ, England.

Copyright © 1990 Usborne Publishing Ltd.

The name Usborne and the device ⌂ are Trade Marks of Usborne Publishing Ltd.

Printed in Spain

About this book

Energy is vital to the world and all the people who live in it. This book explains all about energy and how it is related to power. It looks at all the different forms of energy and how we use them in our daily lives.

There are sections on both traditional sources of energy, such as coal and oil, and also renewable sources, such as the sun and the wind. The book also looks at problems linked with producing energy, for example, the damage caused to the environment by burning fossil fuels, and the unbalanced use of energy around the world. It also examines ways in which we can secure enough energy for the future.

Using the glossary

The glossary on pages 46-47 is a useful reference point. It explains all the more complex terms in the book, as well as introducing some new related words.

Useful addresses

On page 45, there is a list of some of the groups, associations and other organizations you could write to if you want to learn more about energy and power. They will be able to provide you with written material which you can use for projects, and also possibly other addresses you could write to.

Activities and projects

Special boxes like this one are found throughout the main section of the book. They are used for simple activities and experiments which will help you to understand the scientific ideas and principles behind the production and use of energy. All these activities have clear instructions and are easy to do. They all use basic materials.

This scene shows a hydro-electric power station with its enormous dam. It makes use of moving water to turn turbines and produce electricity. The movement energy turns into electrical energy. For more about hydro-electricity, see pages 32-33.

What is energy?

Everything that changes or moves has some form of energy. People depend on energy in many ways — it is what makes things happen. It is used all around us, in transport, in industry and in the home. On these pages, you can find out much more about what energy is and how it behaves.

Below are a few examples of different forms of energy being produced or used. You can find out more about them on pages 6-13.

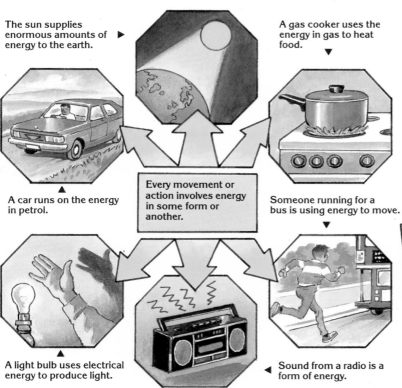

The sun supplies enormous amounts of energy to the earth.

A gas cooker uses the energy in gas to heat food.

A car runs on the energy in petrol.

Every movement or action involves energy in some form or another.

Someone running for a bus is using energy to move.

A light bulb uses electrical energy to produce light.

Sound from a radio is a form of energy.

Stored energy

Energy makes things move or change. The energy in moving things is called kinetic energy. But energy can also be stored in many different things and in a number of different ways. For example, there is a lot of energy stored in things such as wood and coal, and also in food. This energy is locked up in the chemical make-up of the substance, and can only be released when this chemical make-up changes. It is called chemical energy.

Stored energy is released when wood is burnt.

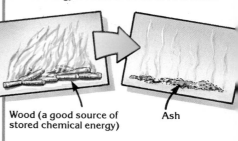

Wood (a good source of stored chemical energy)   Ash

Burning the wood changes its chemical make-up, releasing some of its chemical energy as heat energy (for more about energy changes, see pages 6-7).

People depend on stored energy. Without energy from our food, we could do nothing, not even breathe. Without fuels like wood, coal or gas, most people could not cook or keep warm, industries would not work, and cars, trains and aeroplanes would not move.

Energy is also stored in coiled-up springs and stretched elastic bands. In this form it is called strain energy. For more about this, see page 9.

The coiled spring at the base of the toy has stored energy (strain energy).

When the spring expands, the energy is released as kinetic (movement) energy.

Energy and your body

At this moment, you are using energy in many different ways. You are using light to read this book and heat to keep warm. You are also using energy to stay alive. Without the energy you get from the food you eat, your body would not be able to work. Actions like breathing and the pumping of blood around your body depend on energy.

Your food supplies your body with the energy it needs to do things.

Running   Walking   Talking

Measuring energy

Energy is normally measured in very small units called joules (J). A thousand joules is a kilojoule (kJ). An ordinary-sized apple (100g), for example, contains 150kJ. The same weight of milk chocolate will provide over 15 times as much energy (2,335kJ). Eating too much high-energy food, like chocolate, may lead to health problems. Try to find out how much energy there is in the food you eat. Often the number of kilojoules that a type of food contains is written on the tin, box or wrapper.

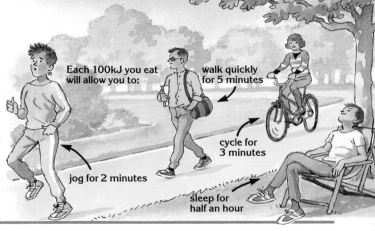

Each 100kJ you eat will allow you to:

walk quickly for 5 minutes

cycle for 3 minutes

jog for 2 minutes

sleep for half an hour

Power

Heat from the coal boiled water to make steam, which powered the engine.

Coal was burnt in the fire-box of the steam engine.

The terms "power" and "energy" are often confused. In the scientific world, the word "power" means only one thing, that is, the rate (how fast) energy is produced or used. Machines are used to turn one form of energy into a different form (for more about energy changes, see pages 6-7). For example, an old-style steam engine turned the chemical energy in coal into movement.

The more energy a machine uses in a certain period of time, the more powerful it is, and the more energy it can provide. A two-bar electric heater is twice as powerful as a single-bar heater. Over the same period of time, it will provide twice as much energy.

The power of a single-bar fire is equivalent to that of seven strong people working very hard.

Measuring power

Power is measured in units called watts (W). A thousand watts make up a kilowatt (kW). Power is the measurement of energy used up in a certain time. One watt is equal to one joule per second. For instance, a 60 watt light bulb uses 60 joules (J) of energy each second (s).

Some appliances are used for longer periods than others. An electric iron is used on average for 20 minutes a day, whereas a television might be on for five hours. The energy used (J) equals the power of the appliance (W), times the number of seconds it is used for (s).

$$1W = 1J/s$$

$$J = W \times s$$

Below are the power ratings of some household appliances.

Electric iron 1000W

Portable radio 10W

Microwave oven 650W

Washing machine 2500W

A matchbox paddle-boat

You can make a tiny paddle-boat with two used matches, two empty matchboxes and a small, thin elastic band.

Place the two matches into the sides of one empty matchbox, pointing slightly downwards. Attach the elastic band loosely between the matches.

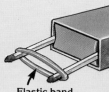

Elastic band

Cut one end off the other matchbox tray, slide it into the elastic band and twist it, so that it winds up the elastic band. Place it in some water and watch it go.

You may have to trim the paddle so it can spin all the way round.

Energy stored in the twisted elastic band is released to turn the paddle and make the boat move forward. This is an example of an energy change (see pages 6-7). The energy changes from strain energy to moving, or kinetic, energy.

Energy changes

Energy exists in many different forms – the main ones are shown here. When something happens, energy is always involved. One form of energy changes into one or more other forms. For example, a battery, when connected up, changes chemical energy into electrical energy (see below).

Forms of energy

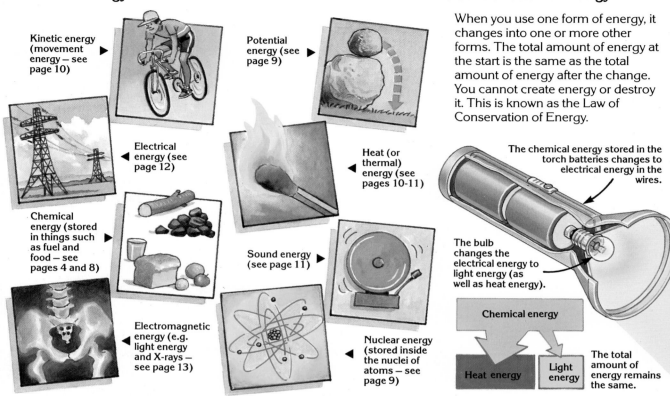

Kinetic energy (movement energy – see page 10) ▶

Potential energy (see page 9) ▶

Electrical energy (see page 12) ◀

Heat (or thermal) energy (see pages 10-11) ◀

Chemical energy (stored in things such as fuel and food – see pages 4 and 8) ▶

Sound energy (see page 11) ▶

Electromagnetic energy (e.g. light energy and X-rays – see page 13) ◀

Nuclear energy (stored inside the nuclei of atoms – see page 9) ◀

Conservation of energy

When you use one form of energy, it changes into one or more other forms. The total amount of energy at the start is the same as the total amount of energy after the change. You cannot create energy or destroy it. This is known as the Law of Conservation of Energy.

The chemical energy stored in the torch batteries changes to electrical energy in the wires.

The bulb changes the electrical energy to light energy (as well as heat energy).

Chemical energy

Heat energy

Light energy

The total amount of energy remains the same.

A funnel record player

Old-fashioned record players show an example of a simple energy change. The loudspeakers on these record players were much less complicated than those of today. You can make something similar using a paper funnel and a needle. You will also need an old, unwanted record and the use of a turntable.

Push the needle through the card at an angle. It should be 2-3cm from the end.

Hold the funnel as still as you can. You should be able to hear the music.

Put the record on the turntable at the right speed. Then place the point of the needle in the groove, making sure that it is pointing the right way (in the direction the record is turning).

Roll a large, square piece of thin card into a funnel and fix it with tape.

Tiny marks in the record's groove make the needle vibrate as it passes over them. The needle passes on the vibrations to the air inside the funnel, producing sound waves. The shape of the funnel concentrates these waves so the sound can be heard more clearly.

The vibrations of the needle make the paper funnel vibrate (kinetic energy), which creates wave patterns in the air (sound energy).

Energy efficiency

The Law of Conservation of Energy states that energy cannot be created or destroyed. However, when energy changes from one form to another, some energy is "lost", that is, it is changed into other forms of energy that may not be wanted.

A light bulb turns electrical energy into light energy. However, a lot of energy is "lost" as heat energy, which is probably not needed.

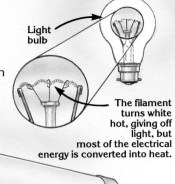

Light bulb

The filament turns white hot, giving off light, but most of the electrical energy is converted into heat.

Fluorescent tube

Energy chains

Energy chains are an easy way to show how energy can change from one form to another, perhaps several times. They can also show how energy is "lost" along the chain. Because of this energy "loss", the amount of useful energy passed on along the chain gets less and less. An example of an energy chain is given below.

Nuclear reactions inside the sun release enormous amounts of energy, some of which travels across space in the form of light (see pages 13 and 14).

Plants use some of the sun's light energy to make their own food (containing chemical energy) which is stored in the plant. Some energy is also used by the plant for its own growth.

When people eat plants, they create their own store of chemical energy. Some of this is used to keep their bodies working, for example, for breathing and moving (kinetic energy). Some is "lost" as body heat.

The kinetic energy used in winding up an alarm clock changes into strain energy in the spring of the clock. Some energy is "lost", due to friction in the moving parts of the clock.

When the alarm goes off, the strain energy changes into mechanical energy (in the hammer). The vibration of the bells produces sound energy. Some energy is "lost", due to friction.

Nuclear energy

Light energy

Chemical energy

Kinetic energy   Strain energy

Sound energy

Machines and appliances are described as efficient if they change most of their energy into the useful form of energy that is needed. For example, fluorescent tube lights are more efficient than normal light bulbs, because they turn more of the electrical energy into light and "waste" less as heat. For more about energy efficiency, see pages 34-37.

Friction is another cause of energy "loss". It is the resistance between two objects when they come into contact with each other, or the resistance between a moving object and the air moving past it.

Friction changes kinetic (movement) energy into heat and sound energy. For example, a car moving on flat ground with its engine off will gradually slow down and stop due to friction.

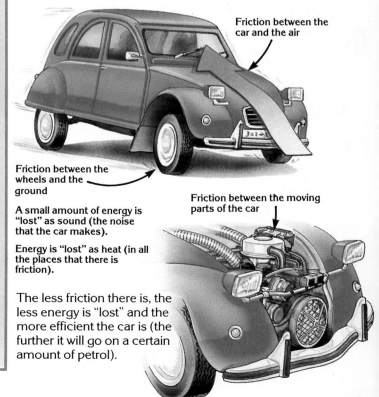

Friction between the car and the air

Friction between the wheels and the ground

Friction between the moving parts of the car

A small amount of energy is "lost" as sound (the noise that the car makes).

Energy is "lost" as heat (in all the places that there is friction).

The less friction there is, the less energy is "lost" and the more efficient the car is (the further it will go on a certain amount of petrol).

Stored energy

The forms of energy on these two pages are all types of stored energy, that is, they are all "hidden", or latent, energy. Under certain conditions, they can all change into other forms of energy (for more about energy changes, see pages 6-7).

Atomic structure

Everything around you is made up of "building blocks" called atoms, which are far too small for the eye to see. In most everyday things there are billions of atoms, yet atoms themselves are made up of much smaller things (subatomic particles) called protons, neutrons and electrons.

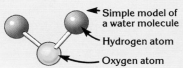

Simple model of a water molecule
Hydrogen atom
Oxygen atom

Nucleus
Electron
Proton
Neutron
Simple model of an atom

A molecule is a group of atoms joined (bonded) together. For example, a water molecule is made of two hydrogen atoms and one oxygen atom. Atoms and molecules are important in stored energy.

Chemical energy

Chemical energy is the energy stored in the chemical make-up of certain substances. It is stored in the bonds between the atoms in their molecules. When these bonds are broken (for example, when a substance burns), some of this energy is released as heat and light.

For example, every methane molecule in natural gas is made up of one carbon atom and four hydrogen atoms. When the gas is burnt in air, the methane molecules break apart. The stored energy is released as light and heat energy. The carbon and hydrogen atoms combine with oxygen in the air to form water and carbon dioxide.

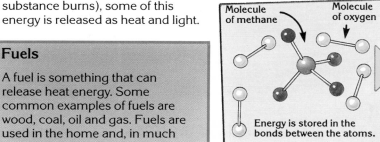

Molecule of methane
Molecule of oxygen
Energy is stored in the bonds between the atoms.

Methane molecule breaks apart when burnt.
Energy released

Molecule of water
Molecule of carbon dioxide

Fuels

A fuel is something that can release heat energy. Some common examples of fuels are wood, coal, oil and gas. Fuels are used in the home and, in much greater amounts, in power stations (see pages 22-23). The food we eat is also a kind of fuel – it is "burnt up" inside our bodies to provide us with energy.

Common types of fuel

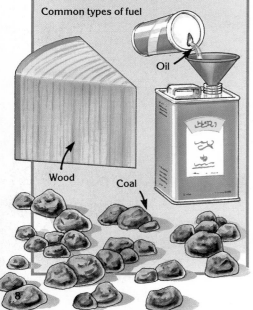

Oil
Wood
Coal

Wood, coal and oil have more complex chemical structures than natural gas, but they burn in a similar way, producing carbon dioxide and water vapour. They also produce more waste products because they are impure (they contain other substances as well as carbon and hydrogen). Coal, for example, produces ash and gases such as sulphur dioxide due to minerals it contains.

Because of their different chemical structures, a certain amount of one fuel will give off more heat than the same amount of another. A certain amount of natural gas gives off more heat than the same amount of oil, and oil gives off more heat than coal.

Power stations using coal and oil produce a lot of pollution.

Sulphur dioxide
Nitrogen oxides
Carbon dioxide

The waste gases they release into the air are partly to blame for environmental problems like acid rain and the greenhouse effect (see page 17).

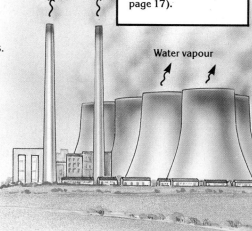

Water vapour

Make your own battery

A battery is a store of chemical energy. The stored energy turns into electrical energy when the battery is used. Inside the casing, different chemicals are stored which react together to create an electrical current.

You can make your own battery using some very basic things. You need one copper-coated and one zinc-coated (galvanized) nail, some thin, insulated wire (about 50cm), a compass and a container of salty water or watered-down vinegar.

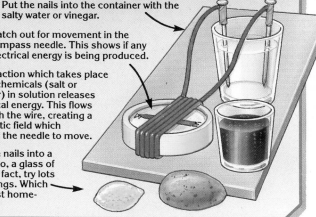

To measure the small electric current that you will produce, you need to coil the wire as many times as you can around the compass, to make a simple meter (you should be able to make more coils than are shown here). Leave some wire at each end.

Attach the compass to a flat surface, making sure the pointer is lined up with the coiled wire.

Strip the insulation from the ends of the wire. Ask someone if you are not sure how to do this.

Twist and tape the bare ends round the two nails.

Tape

Bare ends of the wire

Put the nails into the container with the salty water or vinegar.

Watch out for movement in the compass needle. This shows if any electrical energy is being produced.

The reaction which takes place in the chemicals (salt or vinegar) in solution releases electrical energy. This flows through the wire, creating a magnetic field which causes the needle to move.

Try putting the nails into a lemon, a potato, a glass of fizzy drink — in fact, try lots of different things. Which makes the best home-made battery?

Strain energy

Strain energy is another form of stored energy (see also page 4). It results from stretching or compressing an object, and is the energy an object has because it is "trying" to return to its former shape.

When you wind up a clockwork watch, you are storing strain energy in its spring.

The energy in the stretched (or compressed) spring is slowly released as kinetic (movement) energy to move the wheels and cogs of the watch.

Nuclear energy

Nuclear energy is another kind of stored energy. It comes from the energy that holds together the tiny particles (protons and neutrons) in the nucleus of an atom. There are two ways of releasing this energy: fission and fusion.

Fission

Nucleus of heavy atom (uranium or plutonium) breaks apart, releasing enormous amounts of energy.

This happens inside a nuclear reactor at a nuclear power station, and when a fission, or atom ("A"), bomb explodes.

Fusion

Small nuclei (e.g. those of deuterium and tritium) fuse (join) together, releasing vast amounts of energy.

This is happening all the time in the sun. It also happens when the most powerful nuclear weapon, a fusion, or hydrogen ("H"), bomb explodes.

Potential energy

Potential energy is the energy that an object has because of its position in some kind of force field, such as a gravitational or magnetic field. The example below shows a set of events involving two different forms of potential energy, one caused by gravity, the other caused by a magnet.

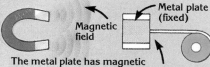

Metal plate (fixed)

Magnetic field

The metal plate has magnetic potential energy. If it were not fixed in position, it would move towards the magnet.

The weight has some gravitational potential energy, because it is in a raised position in the earth's gravitational field. Without the string, it would fall.

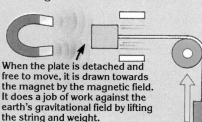

When the plate is detached and free to move, it is drawn towards the magnet by the magnetic field. It does a job of work against the earth's gravitational field by lifting the string and weight.

The weight now has more gravitational potential energy (it is higher up).

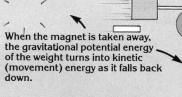

When the magnet is taken away, the gravitational potential energy of the weight turns into kinetic (movement) energy as it falls back down.

For more about gravitational potential energy and kinetic energy, see page 10.

Movement energy

The energy contained in any moving object is called kinetic energy (also known as movement or motion energy). Many forms of energy are based in some way on kinetic energy. The main ones are described on these two pages.

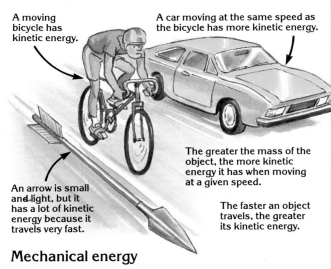

A moving bicycle has kinetic energy.

A car moving at the same speed as the bicycle has more kinetic energy.

An arrow is small and light, but it has a lot of kinetic energy because it travels very fast.

The greater the mass of the object, the more kinetic energy it has when moving at a given speed.

The faster an object travels, the greater its kinetic energy.

Mechanical energy

Mechanical energy is a term that is used to describe several different types of energy. For example, it covers both kinetic energy and gravitational potential energy, and the combination of the two (see below).

A rock balanced on the edge of a cliff has gravitational potential energy because of its position (see page 9). It is capable of doing work.

If it is attached by a rope to an object, using a pulley system, the rock will lift the object some distance when it is pushed over the edge.

When this happens, the rock's gravitational potential energy will change into kinetic energy and the rock's speed will increase:

As it begins to fall, it has mainly potential energy, and a small amount of kinetic energy.

Lower down, more of the gravitational potential energy has changed into kinetic energy, as the rock has speeded up on its way down.

← Pulley system

← Rock

Object

Just before it hits the ground, it has very little gravitational potential energy and a lot of kinetic energy.

At all times, its mechanical energy remains the same, but its form changes from gravitational potential to kinetic energy.

Heat energy

Heat energy is closely connected to kinetic energy, as it is the energy which causes the atoms and molecules of a substance to vibrate (move about). When a substance is heated, its atoms or molecules begin to vibrate more vigorously. When it cools down, its atoms or molecules vibrate more slowly. Heat energy flows from hot objects to cold ones and continues to flow until they are the same temperature.

Heat and temperature

Temperature can be thought of as a measure of the vibration of the atoms or molecules of a substance. However, the amount of vibration caused by a certain amount of heat is different for each substance. If you add equal amounts of heat to identical amounts of two different substances, they will end up with different temperatures. Different substances are said to have different thermal capacities.

Water

Lower temperature

Oil

Higher temperature

Same amount of heat

Oil and water have different thermal capacities.

Temperature is the measure of how hot something is, and is usually measured in degrees Celsius (°C). The amount of heat energy an object can possess is related to its temperature, but also to other factors, such as its size and density.

A red-hot needle has a high temperature, but does not have much heat energy. If it is dropped into a bowl of cold water, there is very little change in the water's temperature, because the needle is so small. A larger object of the same temperature would heat up the water more, because it possesses more heat energy.

Heat energy is measured in joules (J). It takes 4.2J to raise the temperature of 1g of water by 1°C. To heat 10g of water from room temperature (16°C) to boiling point (100°C) takes 3,528J.

Conduction is a way in which heat energy travels in solids and liquids. Heat spreads when the vibration of one atom or molecule is passed on to the next. Some materials, such as iron and copper, allow heat to flow through them easily and are called conductors (they conduct heat well). Others, such as wood and expanded polystyrene, do not allow an easy flow, and are called insulators (they are bad conductors).

Metals such as copper are often used for making pots and pans, as they are good conductors of heat. The heat from the plate reaches the food quickly.

Wooden handles and spoons are insulators. They stop the heat reaching your hands.

Convection is another way in which heat energy can be transferred. When the atoms or molecules of a liquid or gas are heated, they gain more energy and so move more quickly and further apart. The heated liquid or gas expands and becomes less dense. It is lighter, so moves upwards, away from the heat source. The colder, more dense liquid or gas moves down.

The convection currents created by a heater

Hot air rises

Cold air falls

Heaters should be put under windows to heat cold, incoming air.

Radiation is a third way in which heat energy can be transferred. The heat energy travels in the form of electromagnetic waves, mainly infra-red radiation (see page 13). Radiation does not depend on the movement of atoms or molecules, so this energy is the only form of energy that can travel across a vacuum (for example, through space).

A heat-sensitive spiral

A card spiral can be used to show the convection currents of air above a heat source. The energy in the moving air makes the spiral turn.

Cut out a large circle from thin card, and draw a line in the shape of a spiral. The gaps between the lines should be about 1cm wide. You could decorate the spiral with a brightly coloured design.

Carefully make a tiny hole in the centre. Push a long piece of cotton through and tie a knot underneath.

Cut along the spiral with some sharp scissors (be careful how you use these).

Hang the spiral over a heater and watch what happens.

Convection currents are almost invisible, but you can sometimes see them (as a "shaky" effect in the air) above a very hot fire, or above the ground on a very hot day.

The mechanical equivalent of heat

In the 1840's, the scientist Joule worked out the connection between heat and mechanical energy. Using a machine like the one shown here, he measured how much mechanical energy (in the falling weights) was needed to raise the temperature of the water by a certain amount (by stirring it).

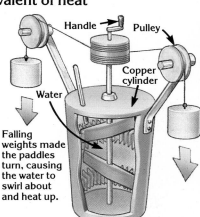

Handle   Pulley

Copper cylinder

Water

Falling weights made the paddles turn, causing the water to swirl about and heat up.

Sound energy

Some opera singers can shatter a glass with the sound of their voice. This shows that sound is a form of energy (because it can do a job of work).

The sound of the singer's voice sets off a wave which travels through the air.

The sound wave moves as particles in the air knock into each other, passing on the energy. These particles have kinetic energy.

The glass resonates with the energy of the sound (the molecules in the glass vibrate at the same rate as the molecules in the air), causing it to crack.

Electricity

We use electricity, or electrical energy, all the time in our daily lives (for more about how it is produced, see pages 22-23). It powers many different appliances, such as irons and cookers, and it can also give us heat and light by making metal wires glow, for example in electric fires or the filaments of light bulbs. The way electricity behaves is connected with the behaviour of the tiny particles called electrons which form part of atoms (see page 8).

Static electricity

Static electricity is the electricity "held" in an object which has an electrical charge. An object has an electrical charge if its atoms have more or fewer electrons than atoms of the same substance would normally have. Most objects have no charge because their atoms have the normal number of electrons. But if they gain or lose electrons, they become charged, and can then attract or repel other objects.

If you rub a balloon against your clothing, you can make it stick to the wall or ceiling.

This is because the rubber in the balloon becomes charged with static electricity, and is attracted to the wall.

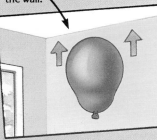

An electrical charge builds up in the base of a cloud.

The flash of lightning is a very powerful electrical spark.

◀ Lightning is a result of static electricity. Water molecules in a cloud rub together with air molecules, creating an electrical charge in the base of the cloud. This is attracted to the earth and the charge (electrons) is released as a flash of lightning.

Current electricity

You can think of an electric current as a flow of electrons. It is measured in amperes, or amps (A). The electrons flow because a force acts on them (an electromotive force, or emf). This force is measured in volts (V).

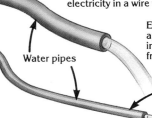

It is sometimes useful to compare the behaviour of electricity in a wire with that of water in a pipe.

Water pipes

Electricity flows when a force is applied, e.g. from a battery. Water in a pipe also needs a force, e.g. from a water pump.

The thinner the wire (or pipe), the harder it is for the electrons (or water) to flow through it.

Electricity travels most easily through metals, such as copper and iron. These are called conductors. It can also pass through water or, if the force is powerful enough, through air as a spark (as in lightning). Some things, such as plastic and rubber, slow down the electrical flow, and are called insulators.

The amount of power (the rate of flow of electricity) is related to the size of the current and the electromotive force. If an emf of one volt causes a current of one amp to flow through a wire, it will produce one watt of power.

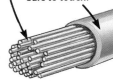

Copper is the metal most often used in electrical wires.

The wires are covered in plastic, which insulates them, making them safe to touch.

$$W = V \times A$$

W = power in watts

V = electromotive force in volts

A = current in amps

Storing electricity

It is very expensive and difficult to store electricity as electricity. Instead, it is almost always changed into another form of energy for storage. For example, batteries are used to store electricity (as chemical energy – see page 9). Another way is to use the electricity to drive a device called a flywheel. The energy is "stored" as mechanical energy.

The current makes the flywheel turn very quickly, turning electricity into mechanical energy.

Some of the energy stored in the flywheel can be turned back into electricity using a generator.

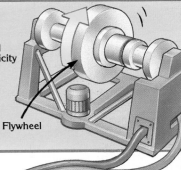

Flywheel

Electromagnetic energy

Electromagnetic energy can be thought of as a combination of electricity and magnetism (magnetic energy). It travels in the form of regular wave patterns. The electromagnetic spectrum is the range of the different, related forms of electromagnetic energy. These have different wavelengths and frequencies (see right and below).

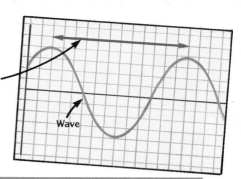

The wavelength is the distance over which the wave pattern repeats itself.

The frequency is the number of waves that occur in one second. It is the number of wavelengths per second.

Wave

The electromagnetic spectrum

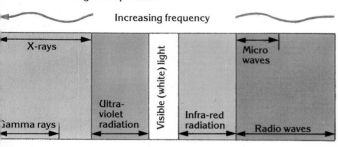

Increasing frequency

X-rays

Gamma rays

Ultra-violet radiation

Visible (white) light

Infra-red radiation

Micro waves

Radio waves

Increasing wavelength

Without the different kinds of electromagnetic energy from the sun (ultra-violet radiation, visible light and infra-red radiation), there would be no life on earth. The sun provides us with light and heat, as well as supplying plants, the basis of life on earth, with the energy they need to grow (see pages 14-15).

The other forms of electromagnetic energy are very useful, too. For example, radio waves are used to communicate over long and short distances. Microwaves are a particular kind of radio wave, and are used in radar (RAdio Detection And Ranging). They are also used in microwave ovens to cook food.

Splitting the spectrum

Visible (white) light is made up of light of different wavelengths (seen as colours). These make up a smaller spectrum within the electromagnetic spectrum. The colours of this spectrum can be seen by passing light through a glass prism. You can simulate this effect with some clear plastic rulers.

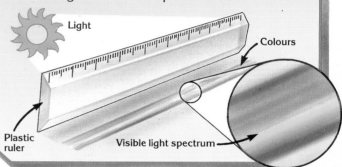

Light

Colours

Plastic ruler

Visible light spectrum

The quality of energy

Some forms of energy are more useful than others – they can be used to do a large number of things, and do them more efficiently. These more useful forms of energy are said to be of a higher quality. For example, electricity is a much higher quality form of energy than low temperature heat energy. It can be used for many more things, such as powering appliances and producing light.

High quality forms of energy can be changed into other forms of energy (for example, electricity into heat) very efficiently, that is, without losing much energy in the process. But changing low or medium quality energy into high quality energy is very inefficient and wasteful (see below and right).

Radar works out the position of an object by sending out microwaves and timing how long it takes for them to come back after being reflected off the object.

Infra-red radiation can be used to make thermal images. These are similar to photographs, but show up areas with different temperatures.

Thermal image of heat loss from a house

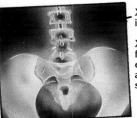

X-ray image

X-rays are used to show breaks and fractures in bones. The rays pass more easily through flesh than through bone, and record an image of the bone on special photographic plates.

Power stations turn hot steam (a medium quality energy) into electricity (a high quality energy).

This is very inefficient — two-thirds of the energy is lost as heat.

In this case, heat is lost in water vapour.

Energy and the earth

The sun produces tremendous amounts of energy, which streams into space in all directions. Some of this energy is captured by the earth. It is what makes life possible on our planet – without it, the earth would be a frozen mass of ice and rock, and no living thing would survive.

The sun's energy reaches the earth in the form of electromagnetic energy (see page 13), the only form of energy that can travel across space. Most of this energy reaches the earth as infra-red and ultra-violet radiation, and visible light. The many uses of this solar energy are described on pages 25-27.

The amount of energy the earth receives from the sun is the equivalent of the energy supplied by over 100 million large power stations.

The sun produces 400 million million million million watts of power.

The sun is over 145 million kilometres away, and its mass is one third of a million times greater than that of the earth.

Nuclear fusion (see page 9) takes place in the core of the sun, where the temperature can reach 14,000,000°C. This releases vast amounts of energy.

Energy in water

Water covers 70% of the earth's surface, and is vital to all living things. It is continuously circulating, in the water cycle, between the surface and the atmosphere, driven by the sun's energy. There is a lot of energy contained in the movement of water. This has been used for hundreds of years, for example in water mills. Today, it is widely used to produce electricity in hydro-electric power stations (for more about this, see pages 32-33).

The water cycle

Heat from the sun makes water evaporate from the surface of the land and sea, forming water vapour.

As the air rises, it cools. The water vapour begins to condense (become liquid again), forming masses of small droplets (clouds).

Energy in the wind

More of the sun's energy falls at the equator than at the poles, so the equatorial regions are much hotter. As it is heated, the air in these regions expands and rises, and colder, denser air rushes in. These air movements cause winds all over the world and influence weather patterns.

Patterns of air movements or winds ▶

The same amount of the sun's energy is spread over a larger area at the poles than at the equator.

Heated air rises (up to 13km above the surface), flows north and south, cools and sinks.

Some air flows back to the equator, some flows to the polar areas.

Cold air flows away from the polar regions.

North pole

Equator

The flow of the air masses is affected by the rotation of the earth.

South pole

The energy of the wind has been used by people for hundreds of years, for example to sail boats, pump water and grind corn. It is now used more and more to produce electricity. For more about wind power, see pages 30-31.

Wherever the wind blows over water, some of its energy goes into creating waves. So these, too, are indirectly produced by the energy of the sun. The energy in waves is one example of the energy in water (see above and right).

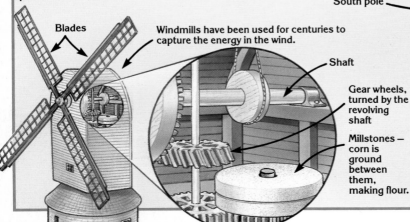

Blades

Windmills have been used for centuries to capture the energy in the wind.

Shaft

Gear wheels, turned by the revolving shaft

Millstones – corn is ground between them, making flour.

As the clouds cool further, the water droplets get bigger. Finally, they fall as rain or snow.

Moving water in rivers has a lot of kinetic energy.

The energy of moving water in rivers is used in hydro-electric power stations. Another type of energy in water is wave energy. You can find out more on page 32 about how this could be used to produce electricity. It may also be possible in the future to produce energy by using the temperature difference between the top and lower layers of water in the oceans (see page 33).

The constant rising and falling of the tides is now also being used to produce electricity. For more about this, see page 32.

Tides are caused by the pull of the moon's gravity and the spinning of the earth.

These create two bulges in the water of the oceans, with troughs (low points) in between.

As these bulges and troughs travel around the earth once a day, they raise and lower the levels of the seas and oceans, creating high and low tides.

The effects of the tides are very slight in mid-ocean, but they are very noticeable on the shores, and especially obvious in bays and river estuaries.

Energy in plants

All green plants take in the sun's energy, as part of a process called photosynthesis, in order to make their own food. This is stored as chemical energy, and used ("burnt") to give the plants energy to grow.

If plants are burnt, the stored chemical energy can be turned into useful heat energy. Fast-growing trees and other plants can provide a great deal of energy in this way (see page 29).

The sun's energy is changed into chemical energy stored in the plant.

When the plant is eaten by an animal, this chemical energy is stored in the animal's body, and then used to keep it alive.

Coal, oil and gas are known as fossil fuels because they are the remains of plants and animals that lived millions of years ago. They are vast stores of chemical energy. Without them, our modern way of life would not be possible. For more about them, see pages 16-19.

The formation of coal (a fossil fuel)

Plants grew millions of years ago. In swamps, they sank to the bottom when they died and did not rot (as there was no air).

Over millions of years, other layers formed on top.

Plant matter turned to coal under pressure.

This is now brought up and used as fuel.

Energy in the earth

The earth itself is a store of an enormous amount of heat energy. This can be seen in volcanic activity, when molten rock (so hot it has become liquid) is pushed up through the earth's crust.

For many years, people in countries such as Iceland, Japan and New Zealand have used steam and hot water coming up from the earth to provide them with heating. These energy sources are now used on a larger scale (see page 33).

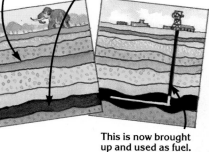

Active volcano

Molten rock, called lava

The layers of the earth (see below) get hotter going down. The inner core is thought to have a temperature of about 3,700°C.

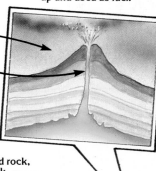

Crust – a thin layer of solid rock, between 6 and 30km thick.

Mantle – a thick layer of hot rock, partly molten, 2,800km thick.

Outer core – a layer of molten metal, 2,240km thick.

Inner core – thought to be a ball of solid metal, 2,440km thick.

The coal industry

Coal is a fossil fuel, formed from plant matter that grew millions of years ago. It is burnt to supply heat energy and, indirectly, electricity (see pages 22-23). Coal is found in many parts of the world, but most is found in the northern half (mainly in China, the USSR, Europe and North America – see page 43).

About 20% of the world's energy comes from coal, and its use is increasing. There are enough reserves to make it an important source of energy for another 200-300 years, but the way we use it at present causes serious environmental problems.

Modern coal mines

There are three main types of coal mine – shaft mines (underground, connected to the surface by vertical shafts), drift mines (underground, connected to the surface by sloping tunnels) and open cast mines (on the surface).

Modern shaft coal mine

One coalface can produce 2,000 tonnes of coal a day.

Tunnelling machine cuts new roadway, so cutting machine can get to new coalface.

The history of coal mining

Coal has been dug out and used for thousands of years. The first real mines (called bell pits because of their shape) were dug in Great Britain in the 12th century.

Early bell pit

The coal was raised using pulley systems or carried up ladders on people's backs.

These pits were never much more than 12 metres deep.

As the demand for coal grew, so did the depth and size of coal mines. This led to advances in mining technology, as problems such as cave-ins and flooding had to be overcome. During the Industrial Revolution in Europe in the 1800's, mining methods improved and more coal was produced.

Coalfaces are often several hundred metres below the surface.

Underground train system carries workers around mine.

Coal cutter moves up and down, and along coalface.

Water cools cutter and damps down coal dust.

Steel roof supports move into coalface as coal is cut (roof falls in behind them).

Studying coal

Find several pieces of coal and inspect them very closely, using a magnifying glass if you have one. Break a piece in half and look inside. You will find that some types of coal break more easily than others, and you should be able to spot evidence of the plants the coal was formed from.

Split piece of coal

You might find tiny, whole fossilized plants.

There are different types of coal, some soft, others hard. They all contain different amounts of impurities (other substances, such as metal ores or sulphur).

Using coal

Coal is used throughout the world to produce energy. Many power stations burn coal to produce electricity – the heat from the burning coal turns water into steam to drive the turbines (see pages 22-23). Many industries, such as the steel industry, burn coal to heat their furnaces. They also burn other coal-based fuels, such as coke. Coal and coke are also burnt in some homes to provide heat and hot water.

Piece of coal

Piece of coke

Coke is made by heating coal to high temperatures without air.

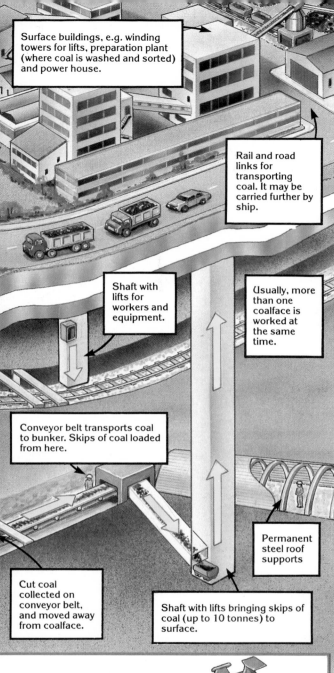

Surface buildings, e.g. winding towers for lifts, preparation plant (where coal is washed and sorted) and power house.

Rail and road links for transporting coal. It may be carried further by ship.

Shaft with lifts for workers and equipment.

Usually, more than one coalface is worked at the same time.

Conveyor belt transports coal to bunker. Skips of coal loaded from here.

Permanent steel roof supports

Cut coal collected on conveyor belt, and moved away from coalface.

Shaft with lifts bringing skips of coal (up to 10 tonnes) to surface.

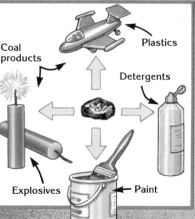

Coal can also be used to make other products, such as tar and industrial chemicals, though the chemicals (which are used to make products such as plastics) are now mostly produced from oil and gas.

Coal products

Plastics

Detergents

Explosives

Paint

Fossil fuels and the environment

The burning of fossil fuels, in power stations and motor vehicles, is causing great damage to the environment. It releases gases into the atmosphere which are partly to blame for the two major problems known as acid rain and the greenhouse effect.

Acid rain

Acid rain is a very damaging mixture of polluting chemicals in rain and snow, produced as a result of burning fossil fuels.

Cars and lorries burn petrol or diesel.

Power stations burn coal.

Sulphur dioxide, nitrogen oxides and hydrocarbons

Chemical reaction in clouds

Sulphuric acid and nitric acid fall with rain.

Kills trees.

Pollutes soil.

Harms plants, animals and people.

Damages buildings.

Pollutes lakes.

The greenhouse effect

The greenhouse effect, also known as global warming, is the gradual warming up of the earth, due to the build-up of certain gases in the atmosphere. Its effects may take another 30 or more years to become obvious, but it may cause polar ice to melt, making the seas rise and flood low areas. It may also alter the world's climates, forcing major changes in farming patterns.

Chlorofluorocarbons (CFCs) produced by industry

Methane produced in nature.

Carbon dioxide released by burning fossil fuels, and burning down tropical rainforests.

These gases let in the sun's short-wave radiation, but stop the earth's long-wave radiation from leaving. This means heat is trapped, as in a greenhouse.

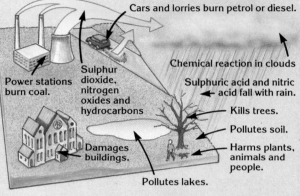

It is very important that we take action quickly to stop this damage. Acid rain can be prevented by using new anti-pollution technology in power stations. Many countries are now doing this, but others say they cannot afford the expensive devices needed.

The greenhouse effect is much harder to solve. Part of the answer is to stop burning so much fossil fuel. This can be done by becoming more energy-efficient (see pages 34-37), and by making more use of renewable energy and, possibly, nuclear power.

Oil and gas

Over 60% of the energy used in the world comes from oil and natural gas, so these substances have a vital role in the world's economy. Oil is the main fuel for transport, and both oil and gas are burnt to produce heat or used to produce other useful substances, such as plastics. The largest underground oil reserves are found in the Middle East. The largest gas reserves are in the USSR.

How oil and gas were formed

Oil and gas were formed from the remains of plants and animals that once lived in the sea. Over millions of years, these remains were buried under mud and rock, under great pressure and at high temperatures. This gradually changed them into oil and gas.

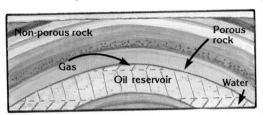

Non-porous rock

Porous rock

Gas

Oil reservoir

Water

Some oil and gas makes its way to the earth's surface and escapes.

Large amounts of oil and gas are trapped below ground in certain areas of rock, forming reservoirs.

Some reservoirs contain only gas.

An oil reservoir is a volume of rock which has spaces in it that are filled with oil. Rock with spaces in it, such as sandstone, is called porous rock. You can imagine a sandstone reservoir as a huge container of marbles, with oil in the spaces between them.

Recovering oil and gas

Geologists work out where there may be oil and gas by studying the rock structure. If oil is discovered, production wells are drilled to bring it up to the surface. Gas and water are then taken out, and it is pumped through pipelines to a refinery.

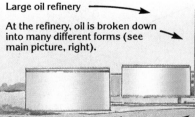

Large oil refinery

At the refinery, oil is broken down into many different forms (see main picture, right).

Oil is transported to and from refineries by pipeline or in large ships called oil tankers.

Oil rig in the North sea

The gas which is brought up is cleaned and treated. Firstly, water and other liquids are removed from it. It is then usually separated and used in various ways (see page 19). If it is to be transported, it may be turned into a liquid (by chilling).

As the oil fields on land are used up, more and more areas under the sea are being drilled for oil.

Rigs at sea have to survive the battering of powerful winds and waves.

About 20% of today's oil is produced from offshore platforms.

Refining and using oil

The crude oil (petroleum) that flows from a well is very thick. Before it can be used, it has to be cleaned and broken down into the different usable forms of oil, in a process called refining.

The different forms are separated in tall columns called fractionating columns. Each form of oil, called a fraction, is a mixture of hydrocarbons (substances made from just carbon and hydrogen). They range from "heavy" fractions (with large molecules) to "light" fractions.

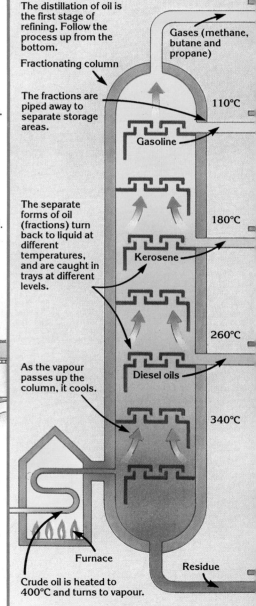

The distillation of oil is the first stage of refining. Follow the process up from the bottom.

Fractionating column

The fractions are piped away to separate storage areas.

Gases (methane, butane and propane)

110°C

Gasoline

The separate forms of oil (fractions) turn back to liquid at different temperatures, and are caught in trays at different levels.

180°C

Kerosene

260°C

Diesel oils

As the vapour passes up the column, it cools.

340°C

Furnace

Residue

Crude oil is heated to 400°C and turns to vapour.

Oil is a useful source of energy for several reasons. As a liquid, it can be stored and moved easily. It is easy to burn and has a high energy density (it has a lot of energy packed into a small volume). The different forms of oil are used in many different ways. The most important of these is transport.

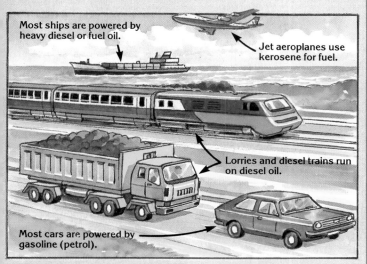

Most ships are powered by heavy diesel or fuel oil.

Jet aeroplanes use kerosene for fuel.

Lorries and diesel trains run on diesel oil.

Most cars are powered by gasoline (petrol).

Heavier oils are burnt in the home for heat, and very heavy ones are used in power stations to produce electricity. Other forms of oil are converted into products like chemicals, plastics, and weedkillers.

Oil spills

Oil spills from tankers or oil rigs can cause a lot of damage to the environment. For example, the Exxon Valdez spill in Alaska, in March 1989, created an oil slick of around 2,400 square kilometres, causing damage that may take ten years or more to clear up. There are a number of techniques used to control this sort of damage. Try them yourself, on a smaller scale, by creating your own oil spill. Tip a small amount of vegetable cooking oil into a bowl, sink or bath of water.

Try to work out the most effective way of controlling or breaking up the spill. Use drops of washing-up liquid to break it up, or drinking straws connected with string, which make floating barriers to contain its spread.

Is it possible to mop up the spill using a sponge or kitchen paper?

Notice how oil sticks to your fingers. It kills seabirds by sticking their feathers together, so that they can no longer keep warm, fly or float.

The uses of gas

Natural gas is made up of a number of very light hydrocarbons, and is a clean fuel, containing no sulphur (one of the main causes of acid rain). After being cleaned and treated, it is usually separated into the different hydrocarbons.

The gas which is piped into the gas mains and delivered to houses and factories is made up almost entirely of methane, the hydrocarbon which is present in the largest amounts. The other hydrocarbons are used in other ways (see below).

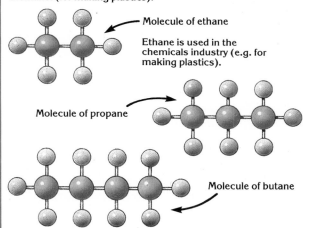

Natural gas consists of methane, ethane, propane and butane (all hydrocarbons).

85-95% of natural gas is methane.

Molecule of methane
Carbon atom
Hydrogen atom

Methane is used for heating and cooking. It is also used to make ammonia (for making fertilizers) and methanol (for making plastics).

Molecule of ethane

Ethane is used in the chemicals industry (e.g. for making plastics).

Molecule of propane

Molecule of butane

Butane and propane are compressed into a liquid known as liquefied petroleum gas (LPG). This is used as a bottled gas (for cooking and heating), to make other chemicals, and as a transport fuel.

A different type of gas, called town gas, can be produced from coal. It is also possible to produce a lot of methane from household rubbish. So even when the reserves of natural gas run out, there will still be ways of producing gas.

When rubbish is buried below ground, it rots, giving off methane gas.

At a landfill gas site, this gas is collected and used (burnt) to provide heat, e.g. for generating electricity. For more about energy from rubbish, see pages 28-29.

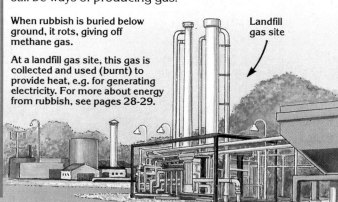

Landfill gas site

Nuclear power

There are about 350 nuclear power stations around the world. They supply almost 20% of the world's electricity. Some of the countries which get an important part of their electricity from nuclear energy are the USA, the USSR, Canada, France, Japan, the UK and West Germany. Scientists once dreamed of a nuclear future with electricity that was "too cheap to meter", but nuclear power has not yet lived up to this, and there are many problems still to be overcome.

Types of nuclear reactor

There are several different types of nuclear reactor, all using nuclear fission (for more about this, see page 9). The most widely used is the pressurized water reactor (PWR), first built in the USA in 1957. The fast-breeder reactor (FBR) is a different sort of fission reactor that actually "breeds" its own fuel (it produces more fuel as a result of its nuclear reactions). But fast-breeders are proving very difficult to develop.

Scientists are also working on ways of controlling nuclear fusion (see page 9) with a view to developing fusion reactors. However, this research still has a very long way to go.

Inside a reactor

In a pressurized water reactor, heat is produced by nuclear fission in the core. The heat creates steam to drive the turbine generators which produce electricity (for more about this, see pages 22-23).

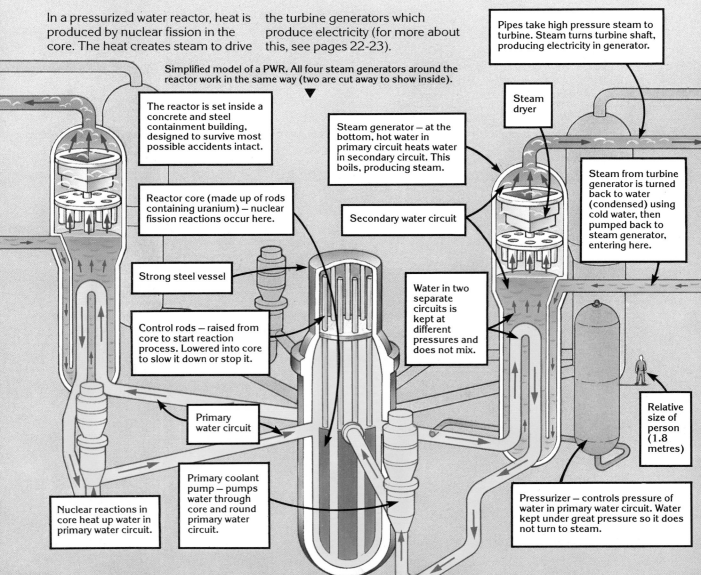

Simplified model of a PWR. All four steam generators around the reactor work in the same way (two are cut away to show inside). ▼

Pipes take high pressure steam to turbine. Steam turns turbine shaft, producing electricity in generator.

Steam dryer

The reactor is set inside a concrete and steel containment building, designed to survive most possible accidents intact.

Steam generator — at the bottom, hot water in primary circuit heats water in secondary circuit. This boils, producing steam.

Steam from turbine generator is turned back to water (condensed) using cold water, then pumped back to steam generator, entering here.

Reactor core (made up of rods containing uranium) — nuclear fission reactions occur here.

Secondary water circuit

Strong steel vessel

Water in two separate circuits is kept at different pressures and does not mix.

Control rods — raised from core to start reaction process. Lowered into core to slow it down or stop it.

Primary water circuit

Relative size of person (1.8 metres)

Nuclear reactions in core heat up water in primary water circuit.

Primary coolant pump — pumps water through core and round primary water circuit.

Pressurizer — controls pressure of water in primary water circuit. Water kept under great pressure so it does not turn to steam.

Nuclear fuel

Uranium is the main nuclear fuel. It is mined in places throughout the world, such as North and South America, India, Africa, Australia and the USSR.

Mined uranium is first purified, and then often "enriched" by adding more uranium atoms of one special type. This type is far more likely to undergo nuclear fission than the other type, which makes up most of the ore. The enriched uranium is made into pellets, which are put together to form rods (see page 20).

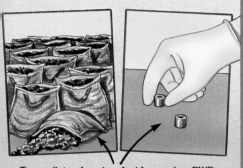

Two pellets of nuclear fuel for use in a PWR are equivalent to 2½ tonnes of coal.

This is enough to produce all the electricity one person in the UK uses in a year.

Radioactivity

Some substances, like uranium and plutonium, are radioactive. This means they are unstable and give off particles or rays, known as radiation.

There are three main types of radiation – alpha, beta and gamma. Each has different characteristics, but all can cause damage, especially cancer, in humans. Neutron radiation is another kind of radiation, found in the core of nuclear reactors.

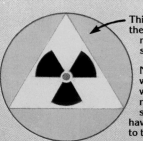

This sign warns of the presence of radioactive substances.

Nuclear power workers must wear or carry meters which show if they have been exposed to too much radiation.

Problems

Power stations using coal and oil are a major source of environmental problems such as acid rain and the greenhouse effect. Although nuclear power is a "cleaner" way of producing power in this sense, it also has its own set of problems. These must be solved before we increase our use of nuclear power.

Radioactive waste

The large amounts of radioactive waste created by the nuclear process cannot be destroyed. Some of it is so dangerous that it must be isolated for hundreds of thousands of years.

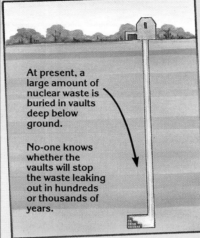

At present, a large amount of nuclear waste is buried in vaults deep below ground.

No-one knows whether the vaults will stop the waste leaking out in hundreds or thousands of years.

Cost

Nuclear power stations are relatively cheap to run, but expensive to build, and there are many hidden costs – such as the costs of research and dealing with nuclear waste.

Accidents

The consequences of a nuclear accident can be many times more serious than those of accidents which occur in other power industries. The nuclear accident in 1986 at Chernobyl, in the USSR, showed this very clearly. It killed 30 people and exposed thousands more to radiation. It also contaminated millions of square kilometres of land.

The damage at Chernobyl could have been even worse if there had been a meltdown.

In a meltdown, the core melts due to the intense heat.

The radioactive material then burns through the containment building into the ground, through the rock, and into the underground water system.

Make up your own mind

You can get hold of a lot of information about nuclear power, and be able to compare the arguments for and against, by writing to electricity and nuclear energy organizations, and to anti-nuclear campaign groups. You could try organizing the arguments in a pamphlet or on a wallchart, and then hold a discussion at school or your local youth centre.

The electricity industry

Electricity is very important to our modern way of living. It is hard to imagine life without it. Electricity is mostly produced in power stations, using large generators. These are usually powered by steam, which is produced by burning fossil fuels or from the heat of nuclear reactions. Some smaller generators, though, are driven by diesel engines, and others by water and wind power.

Generators

A generator is a machine which produces electricity from mechanical energy. The simplest type (for example, a bicycle dynamo) uses the mechanical energy (for example, of the moving bicycle) to turn a magnet inside a fixed coil of wire. Because of the relationship between magnetism and electricity, this produces electricity in the wire.

In a power station generator, the magnet used is a powerful electromagnet. It is turned inside a fixed coil of wire by a piece of machinery called a turbine which is turned by jets of steam. The whole generator produces very large amounts of electricity. The electromagnet itself is supplied with a current to make it work (see page 23).

Many out-of-the-way communities, not connected to a grid system (see page 23), depend on small generators for their electricity. These use diesel engines, instead of steam, to turn the turbine shaft. Places such as hospitals also have back-up diesel generators, in case something stops their supply of electricity from the grid system.

Energy from the sun, wind, waves, tides and flowing water can also be used to produce electricity. These are called renewable energy sources (see pages 25-33).

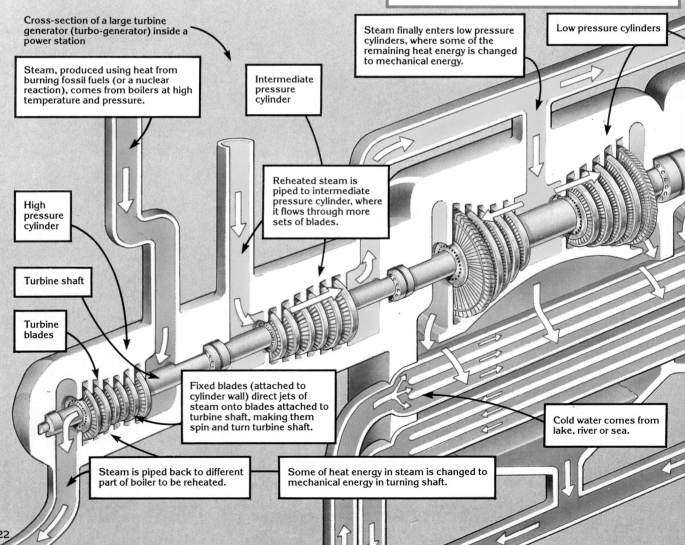

Cross-section of a large turbine generator (turbo-generator) inside a power station

Steam, produced using heat from burning fossil fuels (or a nuclear reaction), comes from boilers at high temperature and pressure.

Intermediate pressure cylinder

Steam finally enters low pressure cylinders, where some of the remaining heat energy is changed to mechanical energy.

Low pressure cylinders

Reheated steam is piped to intermediate pressure cylinder, where it flows through more sets of blades.

High pressure cylinder

Turbine shaft

Turbine blades

Fixed blades (attached to cylinder wall) direct jets of steam onto blades attached to turbine shaft, making them spin and turn turbine shaft.

Cold water comes from lake, river or sea.

Steam is piped back to different part of boiler to be reheated.

Some of heat energy in steam is changed to mechanical energy in turning shaft.

Electromagnets

An electromagnet is a magnet made by coiling a piece of wire around a piece of a certain type of material, such as iron. The magnet can be "switched on" (producing a magnetic field) by putting an electric current through the wire. On page 24, you can see how to make your own electromagnet.

Small electromagnets are used in electric bells.

When the switch is pressed (closed), the circuit is completed. The electromagnet is turned on and the metal arm is attracted.

The hammer strikes the bell.

The movement of the arm breaks the circuit, switching off the magnet (the arm goes back).

If the switch is still being pressed, the magnet goes on again (the process is repeated).

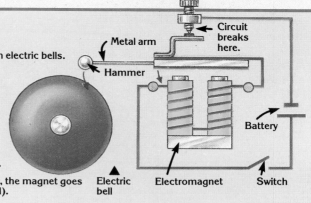

Metal arm

Circuit breaks here.

Hammer

Battery

Electric bell

Electromagnet

Switch

Turbine shaft rotates very rapidly (about 3,000 times a minute).

Turbine shaft is linked directly to electromagnet (rotor) which turns inside fixed coil of wire (stator), producing electricity.

Generator

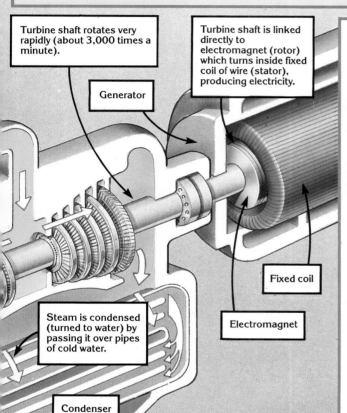

Steam is condensed (turned to water) by passing it over pipes of cold water.

Fixed coil

Electromagnet

Condenser

Condensed steam (water) is pumped back to boiler, to be turned back into steam.

The grid system

Electricity produced in power stations is fed into a network of cables known as a grid. This links the power stations together and carries the electricity to where it is needed – places such as homes, offices and factories. Devices called transformers are used to increase the voltage of the electricity fed into the grid system, and decrease it at the other end (people's homes and places of work). The voltage is the measure of the force that drives the current through the wires. You can think of it as the amount of pressure "pushing" the electricity through the wires.

It is easier, and cheaper, to transmit electricity at high voltage, because less electricity is "lost" through heating the cables. However, it would not be safe to use very high voltage in the home, so it has to be stepped down to a much lower level. Different countries use different household voltage levels (usually 110V or 240V).

Electricity cables are usually suspended from pylons or buried underground, because they carry very dangerous high voltage electricity.

Transformers at power stations increase the voltage from 25,000V to 400,000V.

High voltage electricity cables are made of aluminium (a good conductor).

Saving electricity

If electricity is used carefully and not wasted, then less will need to be produced. This means we will not have to use as much coal, oil or nuclear fuel, and the problems of acid rain, the greenhouse effect and nuclear waste will be reduced. Below are some suggestions for saving electricity in the home.

Turn off lights when they are not in use.

Don't fill electric kettles with more water than you need. They can use a lot of electricity.

Avoid wasteful electrical appliances, like electric toothbrushes. You can brush your teeth better yourself.

Take showers instead of baths. They use less hot water.

For more about saving energy in the home, see page 34.

Making an electromagnet

Electromagnets are introduced on page 23. They are used in power station generators, but have many other uses, too, such as lifting old cars in scrap metal yards. Below you can find out how to make your own electromagnet and switch system.

What you will need

4.5 volt battery
1.5m and 50cm lengths of thin, single-core wire
15cm long iron or steel bolt (or nail)
Switch (paper clip, 2

drawing pins and small block of wood or piece of stiff board)
Paper clips or iron filings
Sticky tape

What to do

Strip 2cm of the insulating plastic coating from both ends of the two wires, using a pair of scissors or a pair of pliers.

Scissors

Wire

Ask for help to strip the wire.

50cm of wire left at the start

Bolt

Always wind in the same direction.

Longer wire (1.5m)

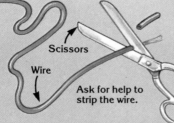

Leaving 50cm free on one end of the longer wire, wind it tightly onto the bolt. When you get to the end, wind the wire back on top of the first coil. Make several more layers, ending up with the wire back at the start.

The more coils you can get onto the bolt, the more powerful the electromagnet will be.

Leave about 30cm free and tape the wire in place.

Tape

When an electric current is passed through the wire, the combined wire and bolt will become an electromagnet.

30cm of wire

To make the switch, first twist the bare end of the 30cm wire from the electromagnet around the point of a drawing pin. Push this, through a paper clip, into the wooden block or piece of board. Then twist one of the bare ends of the second piece of wire (the unused 50cm piece) around the point of the second drawing pin. Stick this into the block of wood 3cm from the other pin and tape the wires down.

Attach the two remaining loose ends of wire to the two terminals of the battery.

Drawing pins

Tape

Paper clip switch in off position

Wooden block

Battery

Terminals

Using your magnet

Your magnet should now work when you complete the electrical circuit by closing the switch. This allows current to flow through the wire. To close the switch, swivel the paper clip so that it touches the second drawing pin.

The magnet should now pick up the paper clips or iron filings. Experiment with other things to see what else it will attract.

Remember to switch off the electromagnet when you are not using it, or it will quickly run down the battery.

Switch in on position

Electromagnet is working.

Iron filings

Paper clips

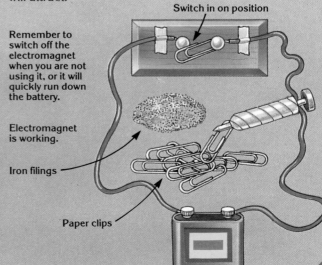

Renewable energy

Renewable energy sources (also known just as "renewables") are those that will not run out. They are constantly renewed in the cycles of the natural world (see pages 14-15) and are likely to play an increasingly important part in providing our energy in the future. The renewables include the sun, winds, waves, tides, rivers and plant matter. On the following pages (25 to 33), you can find out more about these different energy sources.

Solar cells

Wind generator

Renewable sources will be able to provide a great deal of energy, whilst causing far less damage to the environment than nuclear or fossil fuel sources. They do not produce as much waste or pollution, and do not contribute as much to major problems such as the greenhouse effect.

Tidal barrage

Dam

Solar energy

The sun provides the earth with enormous amounts of energy, some of which can be used for heating purposes and to produce electricity. This is known as solar energy, and is one of the main types of renewable energy. Some people believe that solar energy will be the main source of our energy in the long-term future.

Passive solar heating

The sun gives some heat to almost all buildings through their walls and windows. This is known as passive solar heating. The amount of solar energy used in this way can be increased by designing buildings with special features. The ancient Greeks were aware of this over 2,500 years ago.

The ancient Greeks used thick walls for their houses to absorb the sun's heat in the day, keeping the insides cool.

At night, heat stored in the walls kept the houses warm.

These basic ideas have been adapted and improved to increase the amount of useful energy supplied free by the sun. Modern houses, offices and other buildings designed with passive solar features need less heating, and save a lot of money in bills.

This house in Milton Keynes, England shows some passive solar features.

The house is positioned so that large windows on the south side make the most of the sunshine. They have long, heavy curtains to keep out the cold at night.

The house is well insulated (with the methods shown on page 34) to keep the warmth in.

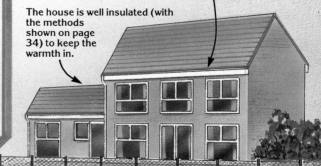

Passive solar experiment

This experiment shows how the sun's heat can be used to heat the inside of a house, and how having a window facing the sun can increase the amount of heat captured. It shows the effects of passive solar heating.

Get two similar cardboard boxes and cut a large window in one. Cover this with plastic wrap, taping it down securely.

Paint each box white or cover them with white paper.

Place a thermometer through the top of each box. Make sure it has a cover (e.g. an upturned mug).

Place both boxes in the sun, making sure the window points towards the sun.

Record the temperatures every ten minutes, and make a graph of the results.

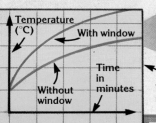

You should find that the box with the window becomes hotter more quickly.

Active solar heating

Active solar heating systems "collect" heat in one area, and then move this heat (using a device such as a pump or a fan) to another area. They are usually used to provide hot water, but can also be used to produce high temperatures for generating electricity.

Active solar heating is more effective in sunny countries. For example, in Israel it produces 90% of the hot water used in houses. The most common solar water heater is the flat plate collector (also called a solar panel).

This form of water heating was first used in the USA in the 1890s. Scientists have since improved on the basic design, by using special glass (to reflect less radiation), different surfaces (to absorb heat better) and vacuum tubes (to lessen heat loss).

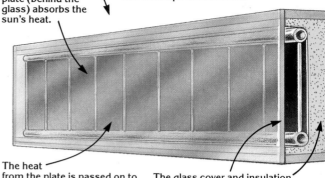

Flat plate collector

Blackened metal plate (behind the glass) absorbs the sun's heat.

The colour black absorbs most of the sun's radiation, and so heats up quickly. White, however, reflects this radiation, and so keeps much cooler.

The heat from the plate is passed on to water running through pipes welded to the plate.

The glass cover and insulation material prevent the heat from escaping.

Making a solar water heater

It is easy to make a simple solar water heater. All you need is a long black hosepipe. On a sunny day, coil this up so that as much of the pipe as possible is in the sunshine (as shown below).

Fill the pipe with water and leave it for about half an hour.

The pipe absorbs the sun's heat and heats up the water.

On a sunny day, the water will get very hot. You could use it for many things, such as filling a paddling pool or washing your bicycle.

Make sure the end is blocked.

Some solar collectors produce very high temperatures, which are used in industry and research, and for generating electricity. Temperatures of up to 3,000 °C can be produced by combining flat mirrors and parabolic (curved) reflectors to concentrate and focus the sun's rays onto a very small area.

Solar furnace at Odeillo, in France

The 42m diameter parabolic reflector is made of hundreds of small mirrors, and is built onto the back of the research institute.

60 flat mirrors concentrate the sun's rays onto the reflector, which focuses them onto a small receiver.

The mirrors track the sun (move round with it), so they always reflect the rays onto the reflector.

Receiver

The heat is used in research experiments in the institute building.

Solar cells

A solar (or photovoltaic) cell turns the energy in sunlight directly into electricity. The most common type is made from silicon, the main ingredient of sand. Solar cells were first developed in the 1950s for use on satellites, but were extremely expensive to produce.

A lot of research into new materials and techniques has gone into the design of modern solar cells. They are now much cheaper and more efficient, and are beginning to be produced in much greater numbers. They are already used quite widely, and for a number of different purposes.

A solar powered calculator includes a solar cell.

Solar cells

Pump

Solar cells powering a water pump in Mali, West Africa.

Solar cells can produce electricity even when the sun is behind clouds.

More solar projects

Below are two more projects which show how the sun's energy can be put to work.

Making a solar oven

The heat of the sun can be used in a simple solar oven to bake food. The instructions here describe how to make one of these ovens. After trying it out, you could also try to invent a larger oven, using the same idea, to bake larger pieces of food.

What you will need

2 polystyrene cups
A large plastic pot, such as a "family size" yogurt or salad pot
Some newspaper
A sheet of black paper
A large sheet of paper or card
Plastic food wrap
Aluminium baking foil
Some food (e.g. sliced carrot or apple)
Sticky tape

What to do

Line one of the cups with black paper, and place the food inside it. Tightly cover the top with plastic wrap.

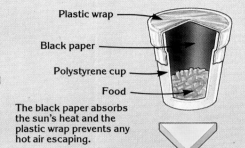

Plastic wrap
Black paper
Polystyrene cup
Food

The black paper absorbs the sun's heat and the plastic wrap prevents any hot air escaping.

Cover one side of the sheet of paper or card with the foil. Make a cone by wrapping this sheet around the cup. Trim it and tape it in place.

Trim here
Tape
Foil on the inside
Paper or card
Cup with food

The foil reflects the sunlight and the cone shape directs it onto the food.

Place the cup and cone inside the other cup, and then place it all in the large pot, packing it with crumpled newspaper or tissue paper (this will insulate the solar oven).

Second cup
Large pot
Tissue paper

Place your solar oven in the sunshine, angled towards the sun, and leave it until the food is cooked. The time this takes will depend on how hot the sun is, but apple or carrot will take about half an hour in bright sunshine.

You may have to move the pot as the sun moves round.

Sun shine
Solar oven

Making a solar still

Solar stills are used in the sunnier parts of the world to get pure water from impure water. You can make a simple version at home, but you will need a very sunny day for it to work properly.

What you will need

Large plastic bowl
Smaller bowl (e.g. a soup bowl)
Plastic food wrap
Small weight (e.g. a heavy coin)
Sticky tape

What to do

Pour 2cm of salty water into the large plastic bowl and place the small bowl in the centre. Cover the top of the large bowl with plastic wrap, fixing it with sticky tape around the sides. Put the weight in the centre of the plastic wrap, so that it pulls it down in the centre.

Place the still outside in the hot sunshine. The water should turn to vapour (evaporate), and then turn back to water (condense) as it cools on the underside of the plastic wrap. The pure water should run down the inside of the wrap, and then drip into the small bowl. To help it condense, you could pour a little cold water on the top (to keep it cool).

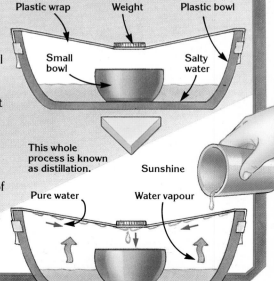

Plastic wrap
Weight
Plastic bowl
Small bowl
Salty water

This whole process is known as distillation.

Sunshine
Pure water
Water vapour

Energy from plants

Plants are the beginning of most of the energy chains on earth. They capture the sun's energy as they grow (see page 7), and animals eat them to create their own store of energy. Living or dead plant or animal matter (organic matter) is called biomass, and the energy it contains can be released and used in many different ways. It is all energy from plants, since the energy in usable animal matter, such as dung, comes indirectly from plants.

Biomass in poor nations

Over two billion people, almost half the world's population, depend on biomass to supply the energy they need for cooking, heating and light. Many of the poorer nations of Africa, Asia and South America get 80% or more of their energy from wood. Another important source of fuel for their fires and stoves is animal dung, which is burnt when wood is scarce or too expensive.

Wood, dung or charcoal is burnt on stoves and open fires that are very inefficient.

A typical three-stone fire, commonly used for cooking in Africa, Asia and South America.

Unfortunately, the burning of wood and dung creates serious problems. The demand for wood has resulted in deforestation. This is when so many trees are cut down that the soil erodes away and the climate begins to change. Dung would normally rot and return important chemicals to the soil, so when it is burnt, less of these chemicals are returned to the soil, which means less food will grow.

Tree-planting, or reforestation, is part of the solution to these problems.

Trees provide a source of energy, shade from the heat, and food for people and animals.

Trees also protect the soil by sheltering it from the wind and rain, and binding it together with their roots.

Charcoal is also widely used in poor countries. It is made by burning wood in a confined space (kiln) with very little oxygen. It is a very useful fuel, which burns at a high temperature with a clean flame and very little smoke. It is easy to carry and use, and is used for heating and cooking in homes in many large cities.

Biomass in wealthy nations

Some of the world's richer countries, like Canada, Sweden and Finland, have large forests and use a lot of wood to supply energy for homes and industries. In most of the other rich countries, though, wood is used mainly for building, and energy is supplied by other fuels. However, these countries are now beginning to recognize the potential in getting more of their energy from biomass.

Refuse

Household and commercial refuse (rubbish) is a major potential source of energy. A lot of it is actually biomass, like paper, food scraps and wood. It can be burnt in special power stations, to produce heat and/or electricity. For example, 20% of the space and water heating in the Swedish city of Malmö comes from burning refuse.

A refuse-burning power station. Trucks deliver refuse, which is burnt on a grate, producing hot gases. The heat from these boils water in a boiler, producing steam which is used to drive turbine generators (as in other power stations — see pages 22-23).

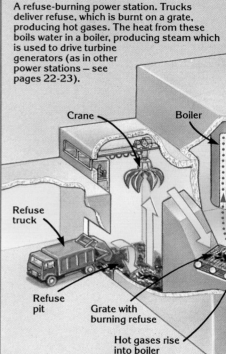

Crane

Boiler

Refuse truck

Refuse pit

Grate with burning refuse

Hot gases rise into boiler

Using old newspapers

Old newspapers can be collected for recycling. Find out if there is a paper collection scheme in your area (contact your local environmental or conservation group). If not, you could turn your old newspapers into a useful fuel source. All you need is the newspapers and some thin wire.

Roll up the newspaper as tightly as you can, so it is about the same shape as a log of wood. Use the wire to tie it up securely. These newspaper logs can be burnt in the same way as logs of wood.

Refuse can also be used to produce energy in other ways. When buried beneath the ground, it rots and produces gases. These gases have been a major nuisance, but they are now being used, particularly in the USA and parts of Europe. They are piped off and burnt for heating or to generate electricity.

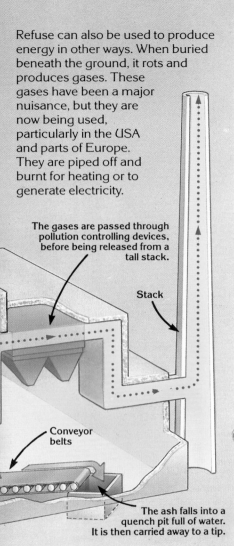

The gases are passed through pollution controlling devices, before being released from a tall stack.

Stack

Conveyor belts

The ash falls into a quench pit full of water. It is then carried away to a tip.

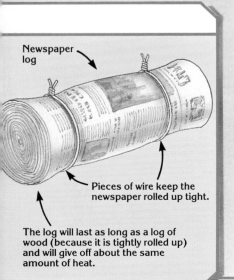

Newspaper log

Pieces of wire keep the newspaper rolled up tight.

The log will last as long as a log of wood (because it is tightly rolled up) and will give off about the same amount of heat.

Waste digesters

Sewage and waste from farms and industries are being used more and more to produce "biogas". The waste rots in containers called digesters, producing the gas. This can be burnt to heat buildings and water.

This makes good use of the waste products, and reduces the pollution they would otherwise cause. Digesters are becoming more common, for example on large farms.

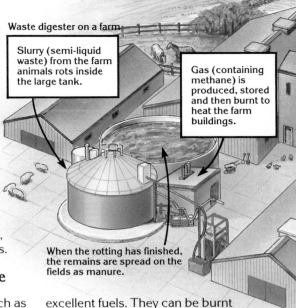

Waste digester on a farm

Slurry (semi-liquid waste) from the farm animals rots inside the large tank.

Gas (containing methane) is produced, stored and then burnt to heat the farm buildings.

When the rotting has finished, the remains are spread on the fields as manure.

Straw and wood waste

Straw and wood waste, such as sawdust and wood chips, make excellent fuels. They can be burnt for heating, or to dry crops.

Small straw-fired boiler

The burning straw heats up water, which is piped around the farm buildings.

Many farms, and some small country industries and estates, such as Woburn Abbey in England, are now using straw-fired furnaces to supply some of their energy for heating. The cost of setting up a system along these lines is soon made up in savings, as the source of this energy is freely available. The straw is burnt in a furnace, which heats water in a boiler. This is then piped to where it is needed.

Enough heat is produced to keep several buildings warm.

Growing fuels

Some fast-growing plants (such as some types of tree) are now being grown on spare farmland, specifically to be cut down and used as a source of energy. These "forest farms" provide an extra source of income for the farmers. One way of raising trees for this purpose is called coppicing.

Certain plants are also being grown to produce different fuels for transport. Sugar cane in Brazil is fermented to produce alcohol, which is used instead of petrol. Other fuels which could be used to replace petrol in the future are also being studied.

Traditional English coppice

The trees are cut off just above the ground and left to sprout.

The new shoots grow very fast because the tree already has a good root system.

The shoots are cut every 4-5 years for firewood and other uses.

Wind energy

The wind is one of the most promising of the renewable energy sources (see page 25). It can be used for a number of purposes, like producing electricity, or pumping water. Many countries are developing wind power technology, especially those whose geography means they get a lot of wind.

Uses of wind energy

The wind has been used for thousands of years to power sailing ships and windmills. Today it is beginning to be used more and more, and for a variety of purposes, some of which are described here. The greatest potential for using the wind is for the production of electricity.

The wind is used on farms to pump water up from under the ground. There are over a million water pumps in use, mainly in the USA, Canada and Australia.

Wind pump ▼

Wind vane — moves the blades to face the wind.

The wind makes the blades rotate. This makes the piston shaft move up and down inside the larger casing, pumping water from below the ground.

Blades

Water

Storage tank

Piston shaft

Water-bearing rock

A few modern ships are being fitted with sails (as well as engines) to harness the energy in the wind. This means they are able to save fuel.

This Japanese cargo ship has two large metal and plastic sails.

A computer turns the sails so they are in the best position to catch the wind.

They can be folded up in very strong winds to protect them from damage.

Making a wind-measuring device

It is quite easy to make a simple device for measuring wind speeds. It will work best where there is a steady wind. You will need two protractors, a table-tennis ball, a flat piece of wood or plastic (such as a ruler), about 15cm of stiff thread, a needle, some sticky putty and some glue.

Thread the needle with ▶ the thread, and push it right through the table-tennis ball. Remove the needle and tie a knot in the thread so that the ball cannot come off.

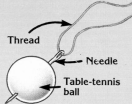

Thread

Needle

Table-tennis ball

Sticky putty

Hang the thread from the centre of the straight edge of one protractor, so that the ball hangs just below the curved edge. Stick the thread on with a small piece of putty or some glue.

Marked sides of protractors

Now stick the other ▶ protractor to the first one with putty or glue, so that the thread is trapped inside.

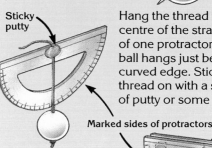

Glue the wood or plastic to the back to make a handle.

If you are left-handed, stick the handle on this side.

Hold the device level, and parallel to the wind (see below). When the ball is blown upwards, read off the angle that the thread reaches, and work out the wind speed from the table on the right.

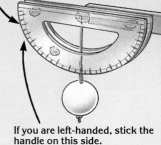

0°

45°

Wind

90°

Angle (°)	Kilometres per hour
90	0
85	8-11
80	12-14
75	15-17
70	18-20
65	21-23
60	24-25
55	26-27
50	28-30
45	31-33
40	34-36
35	37-39
30	40-43
25	44-48
20	49-54

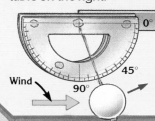

Electricity from the wind

The most important use of the wind is to produce electricity. This was first done in Denmark during the 1890s. Today, it is becoming more and more common.

Wind power has great potential for the future, as it is relatively safe and pollution-free. It can also generate electricity at the same price as fossil fuels and nuclear power.

To produce electricity, the wind is used to turn the shaft of a turbine, which is attached to a generator. This is a smaller version of a power station generator, which is driven by steam (see pages 22-23).

There are two main forms of wind turbine. One type has blades which are fixed on a vertical axis. This means it can catch the wind from any direction (see right).

The Darrieus wind turbine (named after its French inventor)

Small turbines like this are operating in the USA and Canada; much larger ones are undergoing tests.

Wind coming from any direction will spin the blades on their axis.

To generator (which produces electricity)

Turbine shaft

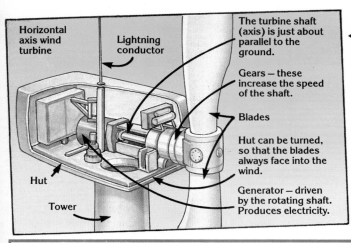

Horizontal axis wind turbine

Lightning conductor

The turbine shaft (axis) is just about parallel to the ground.

Gears — these increase the speed of the shaft.

Blades

Hut can be turned, so that the blades always face into the wind.

Generator — driven by the rotating shaft. Produces electricity.

Hut

Tower

◀ Most wind turbines now in use, though, are of the second type. They have horizontal axes (the shaft is parallel to the ground), which means they must be turned so that the blades face into the wind.

Most horizontal axis wind turbines have either two or three blades, and they differ greatly in size.

The best places to put wind turbines are where the wind is strongest and most consistent, such as on coasts and hilltops. However, this means they are very noticeable, and some people are opposed to them because of this. The machines also make a noise, so they cannot be placed close to houses.

The future of wind turbines

At the moment, there are over 20,000 wind ▶ turbines producing electricity around the world. Most of these are in the USA, Denmark and Holland. Many other countries, like Sweden, the UK, Spain, India and Australia, are developing wind power technology and are building their own wind turbines.

A "wind farm" (a collection of wind generators, producing a lot of electricity) at Altamont Pass, California, USA

There are three very large wind farms like this in California.

Scientists are now designing and ▶ testing bigger wind turbines. Most of those used at the moment are 25-30m high and generate several hundred kilowatts of power, but the new ones can be over 50m high and generate 3-4MW (a megawatt is a million watts). Their blades can be 60-90m in diameter.

There are plans to build large wind turbines out at sea, where the winds are stronger and steadier and where they would be less noticeable.

What a wind turbine at sea might look like.

A project of this kind has many problems, e.g. storm force winds (that could damage the blades).

Legs are driven into the sea floor.

Small wind turbines are important, too, especially for isolated farms and communities. Batteries are used to store the energy produced, for use when the wind is not blowing.

Over large areas, though, the wind is always blowing somewhere. By linking a lot of wind farms to the grid system, electricity can be sent from areas where the wind is blowing to areas where it is not, producing a more constant supply of electricity in all areas.

Energy from water

The energy in moving water is one of the most widely used of the renewable energy sources. It supplies over 20% of the world's electricity through the use of hydro-electric power stations. Other forms of water energy, especially tidal and wave energy, also have great potential, but more research still needs to be done to make the technology efficient and inexpensive.

Hydro-electric power

Hydro-electric power stations use the energy in moving river water to turn one or more turbines, producing electricity in generators (for more about turbine generators, see pages 22-23). Most rivers are capable of powering hydro-electric generators, but less than 10% of this potential is used in poor countries, and only about 30% in most richer ones. A few countries, though, such as Norway and Canada, already get a large part of their electricity from hydro-electric power stations.

Inside a hydro-electric power station

Each hydro-electric power station is specially designed for its site, as no two rivers are the same size or flow at the same speed. The amount of energy available to the turbines depends on two things – the distance (height) between the surface of the water and the turbines (called the head of water), and the rate that the water flows through the turbines.

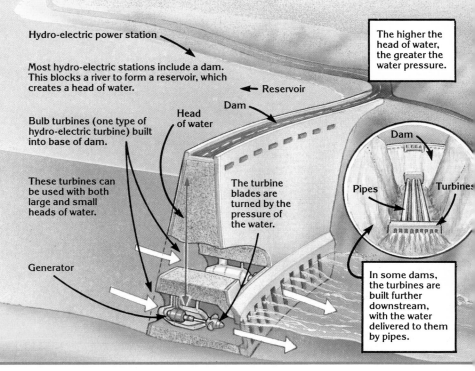

Hydro-electric power station

Most hydro-electric stations include a dam. This blocks a river to form a reservoir, which creates a head of water.

Bulb turbines (one type of hydro-electric turbine) built into base of dam.

These turbines can be used with both large and small heads of water.

Generator

Head of water

Reservoir

Dam

The turbine blades are turned by the pressure of the water.

The higher the head of water, the greater the water pressure.

Dam

Pipes

Turbines

In some dams, the turbines are built further downstream, with the water delivered to them by pipes.

Tidal energy

Turbines like those used in hydro-electric power stations can also produce electricity from the rising and falling of the tide. There are already a number of systems (called tidal barrages) in operation, and several others are being considered, including one across the estuary of the river Severn, in England.

The largest working tidal barrage is in the Rance estuary, in France. Built in 1966, it is 750m long and provides up to 240MW of power.

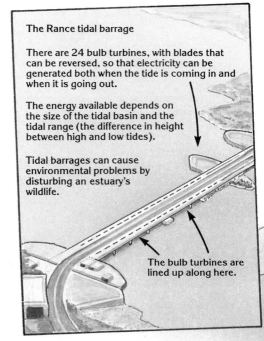

The Rance tidal barrage

There are 24 bulb turbines, with blades that can be reversed, so that electricity can be generated both when the tide is coming in and when it is going out.

The energy available depends on the size of the tidal basin and the tidal range (the difference in height between high and low tides).

Tidal barrages can cause environmental problems by disturbing an estuary's wildlife.

The bulb turbines are lined up along here.

Wave power

Some countries are looking at technology to harness the energy in the movement of ocean waves. This source of energy has huge potential. However, there are many problems to be tackled, such as dealing with high waves and strong winds in stormy weather.

An oscillating wave column, built near Bergen, in Norway (washed away in a storm in 1988)

Turbine blades, with shaft and generator above

Waves moved up inside the column, forcing the air above up through a turbine, generating electricity.

Problems with large dams

Building large hydro-electric dams can cause social and environmental problems.

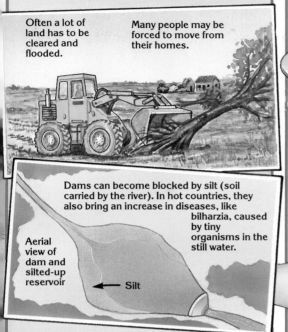

Often a lot of land has to be cleared and flooded.

Many people may be forced to move from their homes.

Dams can become blocked by silt (soil carried by the river). In hot countries, they also bring an increase in diseases, like bilharzia, caused by tiny organisms in the still water.

Aerial view of dam and silted-up reservoir

Silt

Small dams are often a better choice than large ones, especially for supplying power to country areas. They cause less damage, and are easier to build. Almost 100,000 have been built in China since 1968 (providing over 5,000MW of power).

Making a water wheel

Water wheels have been used for centuries to use the energy in moving water to do work.

Below is an example of a simple model water wheel you can make with basic materials.

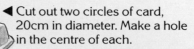

◀ Cut out two circles of card, 20cm in diameter. Make a hole in the centre of each.

Cut up two egg cartons to make 12 small buckets. Paint or varnish these to make the outsides waterproof.

Stick or staple the buckets to the card, ▶ making the water wheel.

Place a 15cm nail through the holes in the card.

Tie some string very tightly to the nail and attach a weight (such as a pencil) to the end.

Buckets attached to card circles

Open ends should face outwards.

To attach the wire, make loops at both ends.

◀ Use a piece of wood (such as a ruler) and some wire to support the nail.

Put the wheel under a tap and watch it lift the weight.

Experiment with different water speeds from the tap.

OTEC

In hot, equatorial areas there is another potential means of gaining energy from the oceans, by using the temperature difference between the layers of water. The method, still being researched at present, is called Ocean Thermal Energy Conversion (OTEC).

OTEC devices use warm surface water to heat up and vaporize a fluid with a low boiling point, such as ammonia. The moving vapour drives a turbine, generating electricity. Cold water from deeper down is then used to cool the vapour and condense it back to ammonia for recirculating.

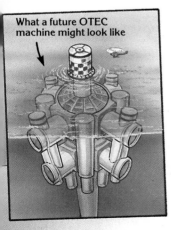

What a future OTEC machine might look like

Geothermal energy

Heat which comes from the earth itself is called geothermal energy. It is already used in some parts of the world, such as Iceland, where natural steam is produced as water passes over hot rock under the earth's surface. This steam is used to generate electricity.

Elsewhere, such as in France, warm water is pumped up from underground to heat blocks of flats.

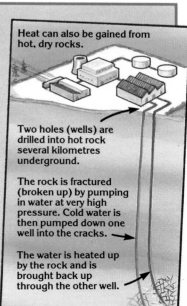

Heat can also be gained from hot, dry rocks.

Two holes (wells) are drilled into hot rock several kilometres underground.

The rock is fractured (broken up) by pumping in water at very high pressure. Cold water is then pumped down one well into the cracks.

The water is heated up by the rock and is brought back up through the other well.

Energy efficiency

Being energy-efficient means continuing to do most of the things we do today, but using less energy to do them. If we save energy, less is needed, and we reduce the damage to the environment caused by producing energy. Being energy-efficient is the cheapest and simplest way to start solving serious environmental problems. On the next four pages, you can find out about saving energy.

You may not be in a position yourself to make many of the changes suggested, but if you know about them you can make other people aware of them.

Saving energy in the home

Many buildings, especially old ones, are very inefficient to heat, because they lose so much heat to the outside environment. By introducing a number of simple energy saving (conservation) measures, the cost of heating these buildings can often be cut by a half.

This shows where heat is lost from a house in winter, and how this heat loss can be reduced.

If you turn your heating down by a few degrees, you can save a lot of energy, and you probably won't notice the difference.

Insulating your hot water tank will make it heat up more quickly and stay hot for longer.

There are some more energy-saving ideas on page 23.

These energy-saving measures can also be used in larger buildings, such as schools and offices. Here, the amount of energy and money that can be saved is quite large. Find out if your school or community centre can put some of these measures into action. You could do your bit to help.

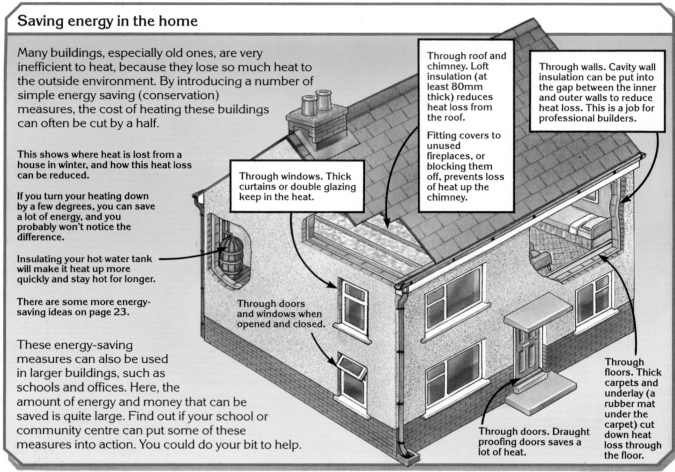

Through roof and chimney. Loft insulation (at least 80mm thick) reduces heat loss from the roof.

Fitting covers to unused fireplaces, or blocking them off, prevents loss of heat up the chimney.

Through walls. Cavity wall insulation can be put into the gap between the inner and outer walls to reduce heat loss. This is a job for professional builders.

Through windows. Thick curtains or double glazing keep in the heat.

Through doors and windows when opened and closed.

Through doors. Draught proofing doors saves a lot of heat.

Through floors. Thick carpets and underlay (a rubber mat under the carpet) cut down heat loss through the floor.

Efficient heating

As well as preventing heat loss, it is important to make sure that the type of heating you use is as efficient as possible. There have been many developments in heating efficiency over the years, which have saved a great deal of energy and money for the people who have used them. Much more could still be done, though. The efficiency of a heating system varies according to the type of fuel it uses, whether it is in good or bad condition, and how sensibly it is used.

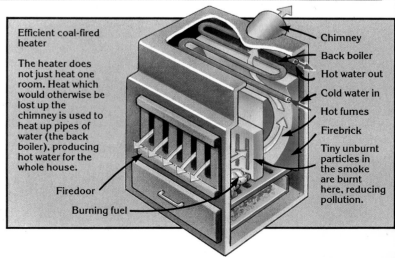

Efficient coal-fired heater

The heater does not just heat one room. Heat which would otherwise be lost up the chimney is used to heat up pipes of water (the back boiler), producing hot water for the whole house.

Chimney

Back boiler

Hot water out

Cold water in

Hot fumes

Firebrick

Tiny unburnt particles in the smoke are burnt here, reducing pollution.

Firedoor

Burning fuel

Supplying energy to homes

One of the most efficient ways to provide heating in towns and cities where buildings are close together is known as district, or community, heating. Instead of each house and office burning fuel to provide its own heating, the heat for all the buildings is produced at a central point (such as a boiler or a power station).

Power stations which produce both electricity and district heating are called combined heat and power (CHP) stations. For more about CHP, see page 36.

CHP station in Denmark →

Household appliances

There are big differences in the energy efficiency of different makes of electrical appliance (such as fridges, cookers and irons). Your family can save a lot of electricity, and money, by using the ones that are the most energy-efficient. Ask about the energy efficiency of different models when you are in the shop to make sure your parents buy the most efficient.

Some fridges now on sale use only a fifth of the electricity used by other fridges of the same size, and some now being developed will use just a tenth.

If everyone in the UK who bought a fridge in the next 15 years bought the most efficient type, the total saving would be 1,800MW (the power of 2 nuclear reactors).

Slow cookers

A very energy-efficient way of cooking is to use a slow cooker – a large, well-insulated casserole dish which plugs into the mains and cooks food for 6-8 hours, using very little energy. Slow cooking itself is a very old cooking method, and is an excellent way to cook casseroles and soups. You can make an old-style slow cooker (a haybox cooker) very easily.

How to make and use a haybox cooker

Get a cardboard box that is large enough to fit a saucepan inside, with space around it.

Fill the box tightly with dry hay or straw, leaving a hole big enough for the saucepan.

Put the ingredients in the saucepan, put the lid on, and boil for 10 minutes (it is important to get the food very hot to start with). Then put the pan into the hole in the haybox, and cover it with another tightly-packed layer of hay or straw.

Close the flaps on the top of the box, and seal them with tape.

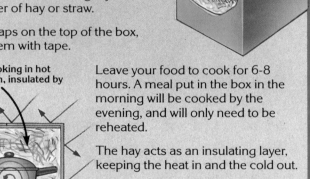

Food cooking in hot saucepan, insulated by haybox →

Leave your food to cook for 6-8 hours. A meal put in the box in the morning will be cooked by the evening, and will only need to be reheated.

The hay acts as an insulating layer, keeping the heat in and the cold out.

You could try other insulating materials, such as crumpled-up newspaper or polystyrene.

Energy efficient stoves

Many people in poor countries are not able to afford modern cooking and heating appliances, or the fuel that they burn. Many still burn wood on open fires and stoves, but, as more and more trees are cut down for fuel, whole areas are becoming deforested (losing all their trees).

This situation would improve if the open fires were replaced by low cost, energy-efficient ones, but care must be taken not to disrupt the people's way of life. Open stoves not only give them heat, but also lighting at night. They are also important as the centre of family life.

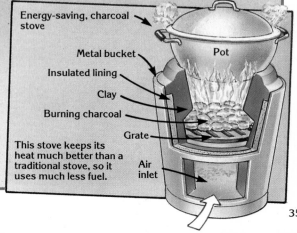

Energy-saving, charcoal stove

Pot

Metal bucket

Insulated lining

Clay

Burning charcoal

Grate

Air inlet

This stove keeps its heat much better than a traditional stove, so it uses much less fuel.

Efficiency in industry

Many of the basic energy-saving measures used in the home can also be used in buildings where people work. The buildings and machinery used in industry, however, are much larger and more complex, so there are also different problems to be faced in order to improve energy efficiency. There are a number of ways to solve these problems, and these need to be used more widely.

The heat wheel

The heat wheel is an energy-saving device used in industry. It uses the heat from warm air or hot fumes leaving a building or factory to warm up fresh, incoming air. A heat wheel recovers up to 80% of the heat in the outgoing air, saving a lot of energy.

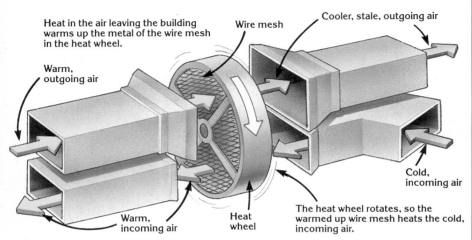

Heat in the air leaving the building warms up the metal of the wire mesh in the heat wheel.

Wire mesh

Cooler, stale, outgoing air

Warm, outgoing air

Cold, incoming air

Warm, incoming air

Heat wheel

The heat wheel rotates, so the warmed up wire mesh heats the cold, incoming air.

People in industry and business should be encouraged to introduce energy-saving devices and techniques to old buildings, or add them to new ones as they are built. They may be expensive to buy, but they can save money, as well as energy, in the long term.

Combined heat and power

One important place to improve efficiency is in large power stations which use coal or oil. Only about 35% of the energy put in as fuel is converted into electricity. The rest is lost as heat. In the UK, for example, the heat lost from power stations is enough to heat every home in the country.

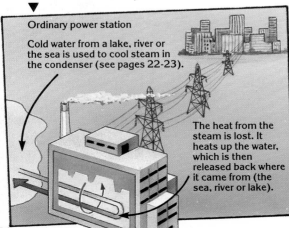

Ordinary power station

Cold water from a lake, river or the sea is used to cool steam in the condenser (see pages 22-23).

The heat from the steam is lost. It heats up the water, which is then released back where it came from (the sea, river or lake).

Combined heat and power (CHP) stations produce electricity and useful heat at the same time. Instead of being released, hot water from the production of electricity is piped to local buildings and used for space and water heating. This is known as district heating.

CHP stations produce slightly less electricity than ordinary power stations. But they use more of the heat produced, and can be twice as efficient overall (70-80% efficient).

Embedded energy

In many industries, a lot of energy is used to make materials and goods — for example, to heat the furnaces in which steel and glass are made. This energy is sometimes known as embedded energy. If the materials, and the things which are made from them, are repaired, recycled and used again, then less energy needs to be used up in producing more materials and goods.

Any substance that is made using a lot of energy, such as steel or glass, has a lot of embedded energy.

Car

Glass windscreen and windows

Steel body

Any object that is made from these substances, such as a car, also has a lot of embedded energy.

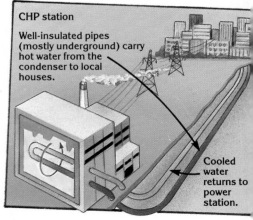

CHP station

Well-insulated pipes (mostly underground) carry hot water from the condenser to local houses.

Cooled water returns to power station.

There are also much smaller CHP generators which produce both electricity and heat in the same way as the larger ones. These can be used in all kinds of industrial buildings.

Efficiency in transport

About a quarter of all the energy used in some industrialized nations is used in transport. However, many means of transport are very inefficient, both as machines and as ways of carrying people and goods. By using new technology, we could produce machines which are more energy-efficient. Also, by changing our ideas about the way we use transport, we could create better, more energy-efficient transport systems and a more pleasant, less polluted environment.

More efficient cars

Most cars are inefficient in the way they use energy. In the average car engine, only about 15% of the chemical energy stored in petrol is actually converted into the movement energy of the car. The rest is lost as heat. Engineers are now working on new, more efficient cars and engines for the future.

A more energy-efficient car of the future ▶

Streamlined car body means there is less friction between the air and the car. The air flows more smoothly over the body, so less energy has to be used up in moving against it.

Lighter bodywork (perhaps made of strong, hard plastic) means the engine has to do less work (it has to move less weight) and so uses up less energy.

Smaller, more efficient engine (converts more of the chemical energy in petrol into movement energy).

Cars and public transport

Although cars can be very useful, even energy-saving cars can be an inefficient means of transport. This is especially true in crowded areas, such as towns and cities. A car takes up road space and uses up a lot of energy, often to carry just one person.

As more cars are bought, traffic-jams threaten to bring many large cities to a standstill.

Some cities, like San Francisco in the USA, are now introducing laws to reduce the number of private cars allowed on the streets.

Public transport is a much more energy-efficient way to move people around. Many people would like to see private cars banned from city centres, and replaced by much better public transport systems, with cheap, regular and extensive services. This would also reduce pollution from exhausts.

The number of heavy lorries on the roads could also be reduced, by introducing better rail systems. Trains are more energy-efficient for moving people and goods over long distances.

Riding a bicycle

The bicycle is a very efficient machine. It takes little energy to travel comfortably over quite long distances. More people are now using bicycles, both for enjoyment and to keep fit. By not using petrol, they help to save energy and reduce air pollution. Below are some ideas to help make a bicycle work more efficiently.

Keep the tyres well pumped up. A flat tyre has more surface touching the road. This causes friction and slows you down.

Keep the moving parts well oiled. Oil reduces friction, making it easier to ride.

Oil at the points labelled below.
▼

Make sure the bicycle is the right size for you and the seat is at the correct height. If not, it will be harder to cycle (your leg muscles will not be working as efficiently as they could).

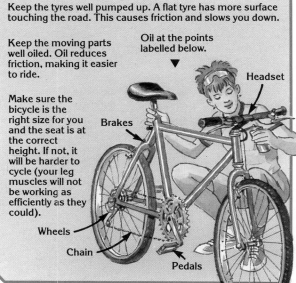

Headset

Brakes

Wheels

Chain

Pedals

Energy in the future

Within the next few decades, there will have to be great changes in the way energy is used throughout the world. The way we produce and use energy at the moment is causing serious damage to the environment. At the same time, demand for energy is increasing as the world's population continues to grow, but there are only limited reserves of fossil fuels, which today provide about 80% of the world's energy. It is very important that everyone begins to use energy carefully and responsibly.

The growth of pollution

When coal was first burnt in large quantities, during the Industrial Revolution in Europe in the 1800s, the pollution produced was mostly local. Towns and cities became very dirty and unhealthy.

Smog was a result of smoke from coal fires and factories mixing with fog.

Smog (a mixture of smoke and fog) in a large city in the 1870s.

Many people used to die from bronchitis and asthma when the smog was particularly bad.

Tall smoke stacks release pollution high above the ground, where strong winds carry it away, often for hundreds of miles.

Norway

Prevailing winds

Acid rain damages trees and lakes.

Britain

Later, steps were taken to get rid of smog. Smokeless fuels were introduced and tall smoke stacks were built at power stations and factories to carry smoke away from local areas. But this meant that pollution was spread much further afield. For example, trees and lakes in Norway have been damaged by pollution from British power stations.

As they grew wealthier, the industrialized countries burnt larger amounts of fossil fuels. This has resulted in a gradual build up of carbon dioxide in the atmosphere, which is one of the main causes of the greenhouse effect. This is a serious threat to the world's environment, and pollution has now become an international problem.

Energy use in rich countries

In most rich countries, people's lifestyles are very wasteful of energy. This is because modern lifestyles developed when energy was cheap and plentiful, and few people realized the dangers of pollution. But we now know about these dangers, and can see that some of our energy resources will soon become more scarce. Because of these things, we must begin to change the way we use energy.

Some people believe that more and more energy must be used to improve living standards. However, this is only true in countries which are still building up their industries. In nations with a lot of modern industries, there is a much less direct link between energy use and living standards.

In the USA, the large, "gas-guzzling" car used to be very common. Today, far more Americans drive smaller, more energy-efficient cars.

In Japan, the standard of living has continued to improve without an increase in energy use.

Japan used the same amount of energy in 1984 as it did in 1979, but there was a 23% increase in the country's wealth.

A lot of energy is saved by recycling materials and increasing energy efficiency.

An energy-efficient high-speed train in Japan

Energy use in poor countries

Many of the world's poorest countries have very large, growing populations, but their use of energy sources per person is low compared to the rich countries.

However, a number of these countries have plenty of coal and want to develop their industries in the same way as the rich countries have, to improve the standard of living of their people. This would mean a vast increase in energy use and world pollution, and would greatly speed up the rate at which world resources are used up.

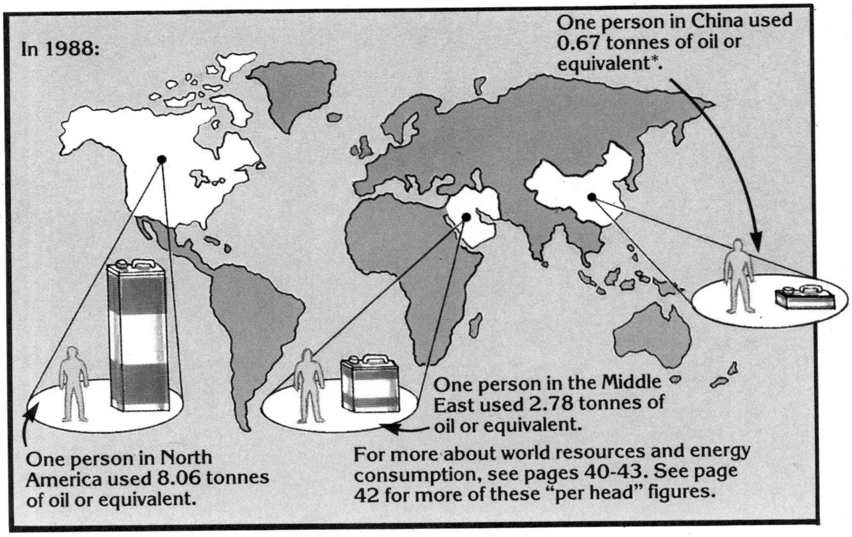

In 1988:
One person in China used 0.67 tonnes of oil or equivalent*.
One person in the Middle East used 2.78 tonnes of oil or equivalent.
One person in North America used 8.06 tonnes of oil or equivalent.

For more about world resources and energy consumption, see pages 40-43. See page 42 for more of these "per head" figures.

Changes in energy use

Every few years something dramatic happens which changes the way people think about energy. These events affect the choices governments make about how to use energy in the future. For example, in 1973, the main oil-producing nations quadrupled the price of oil and threatened to stop supplying it to some countries. Then, in 1985, prices collapsed due to over-production. Another example is the nuclear accident at Chernobyl in the USSR in 1986, which changed many people's minds about the safety of nuclear power.

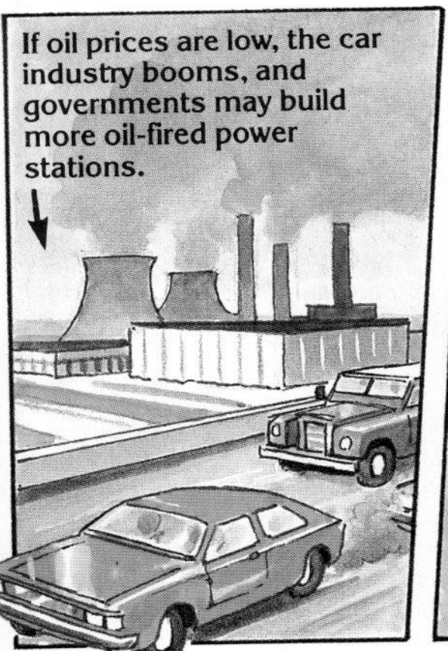

If oil prices are low, the car industry booms, and governments may build more oil-fired power stations.

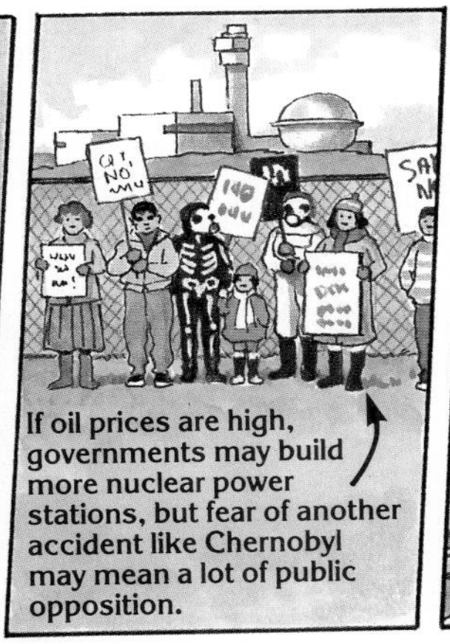

If oil prices are high, governments may build more nuclear power stations, but fear of another accident like Chernobyl may mean a lot of public opposition.

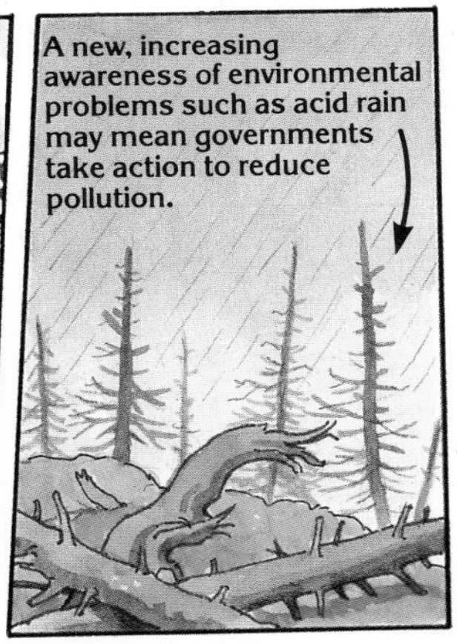

A new, increasing awareness of environmental problems such as acid rain may mean governments take action to reduce pollution.

Scientific discoveries are also unpredictable. For example, newly-developed substances called high temperature superconductors, which conduct electricity very efficiently, are likely to improve greatly the efficiency of machines and cables. Events like these will continue to happen, making long-term planning very difficult.

Solutions to the energy question

We are surrounded by sources of energy that can be used to make our lives more comfortable and enjoyable. But all energy sources have a cost, in terms of money and environmental damage. If they are used sensibly, we can continue to have enough energy without destroying our environment. To achieve this, we will have to make some changes, such as those suggested here.

The wealthy ▶ countries must reduce their energy use, perhaps by 50% by the year 2020, by being more energy-efficient.

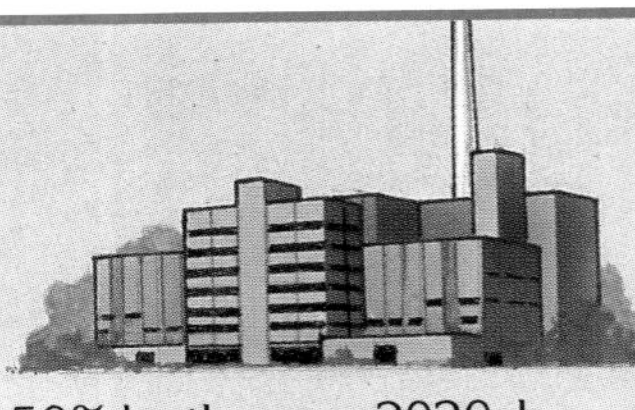

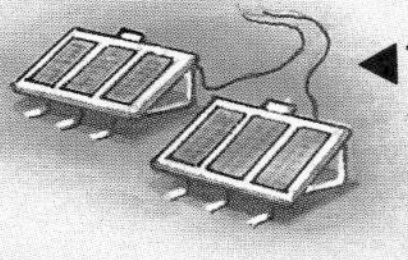

◀ They must also share their knowledge and technology with the poor countries, to help them develop their own efficient and appropriate ways of producing energy.

Laws must be passed, and help given, to make sure anti-pollution technology is introduced and used in all countries.

There must be more ▶ co-operation to tackle world problems such as the greenhouse effect.

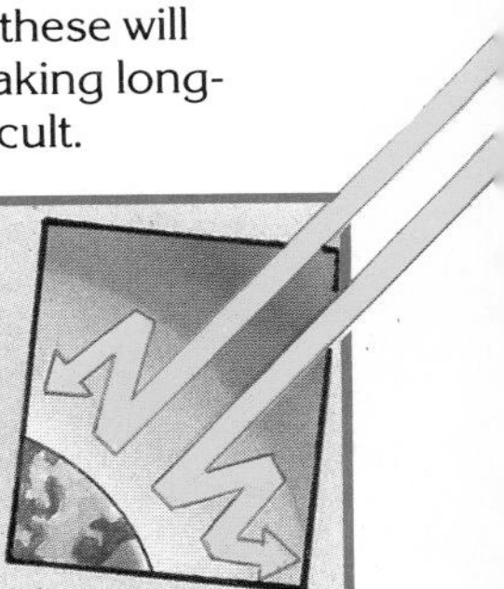

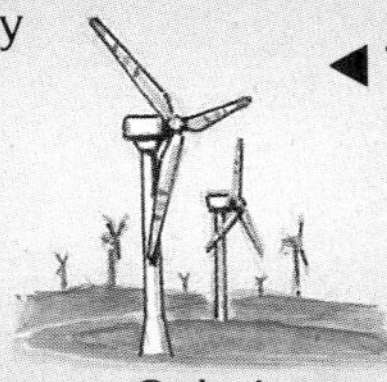

◀ There must be more research into renewable sources of energy, and a gradual switch away from fossil fuels to these cleaner, safer sources.

Solutions must be found to the problems of nuclear waste and the safety of nuclear reactors, before there is a further increase in the use of nuclear power around the world. ▼

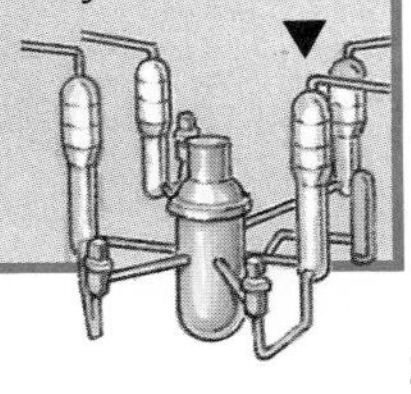

*See pages 40 and 41 for an explanation of "oil equivalent".

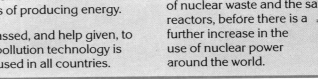

World energy facts

On the next four pages there are some charts, maps and graphs which give an idea of the different amounts of energy produced and consumed in different areas of the world, and also the estimated reserves of these sources around the world.

Production and consumption of fossil fuels

The charts below give the amounts of oil, natural gas and coal produced (brought out of the ground to be used or sold) and consumed (used) by different areas of the world in 1988.

Each area is a group of countries (the groups are standard groups used in such statistics). If the figure for a particular country within a group is significantly larger than the figures of the other countries in that group, then it is given separately.

Oil production, 1988 (million tonnes**)

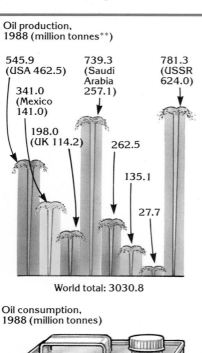

545.9 (USA 462.5)

341.0 (Mexico 141.0)

198.0 (UK 114.2)

739.3 (Saudi Arabia 257.1)

262.5

135.1

27.7

781.3 (USSR 624.0)

World total: 3030.8

Oil consumption, 1988 (million tonnes)

863.9 (USA 789.2)

228.1

596.6 (West Germany 114.8)

135.4

429.1 (Japan 222.2)

664.9 (USSR 439.1)

86.2

34.3

World total: 3038.5

The figures for gas and coal are given in units called "million tonnes of oil equivalent" ("mtoe"). These figures are arrived at by working out how much energy would be, or was, obtained from the total amount of gas or coal, and then giving the number of millions of tonnes of oil that would produce the same amount of energy.

Natural gas production, 1988 (mtoe)

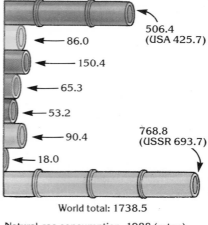

506.4 (USA 425.7)

86.0

150.4

65.3

53.2

90.4

18.0

768.8 (USSR 693.7)

World total: 1738.5

Natural gas consumption, 1988 (mtoe)

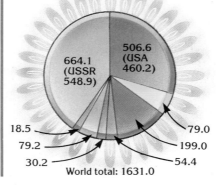

664.1 (USSR 548.9)

506.6 (USA 460.2)

18.5

79.2

30.2

79.0

199.0

54.4

World total: 1631.0

Coal production, 1988 (mtoe)

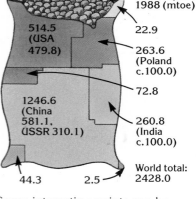

570.0 (USA 524.3)

21.2

186.8 (Poland 142.4)

100.0

1329.2 (China 579.2, USSR 391.9)

145.6 (India 121.9)

90.3

(Middle East 0.7)

World total: 2443.8

Coal consumption, 1988 (mtoe)

514.5 (USA 479.8)

22.9

263.6 (Poland c.100.0)

72.8

1246.6 (China 581.1, USSR 310.1)

260.8 (India c.100.0)

44.3

2.5

World total: 2428.0

Some interesting points can be made from looking at figures such as these. For instance, countries such as the USA consume far more oil than they produce. These countries must rely on buying oil from other countries. Also, you can see that the top five coal producers (the countries named) are also the top five consumers.

* Albania, Bulgaria, China, Cuba, Czechoslovakia, East Germany, Hungary, Kampuchea, Laos, Mongolia, North Korea, Poland, Romania, USSR, Vietnam, Yugoslavia.
** One tonne (metric ton) = 1,000 kilograms or 0.98 tons (imperial tons)

Nuclear and hydro-electric energy

Most of the world's energy comes from burning fossil fuels. But some energy is also produced by nuclear power stations and the various renewable sources. A complete picture of energy consumption is not possible without figures for these sources, but unfortunately some figures are incomplete and unreliable, in particular those for the burning of wood in Third World countries (in many cases, the main source of energy in these countries). The only clear international figures available for non-fossil sources are for electricity obtained from nuclear and hydro-electric power. As before, mtoe units are used, in this case being the amount of oil which would fuel an oil-fired power station to produce the same amount of electricity.

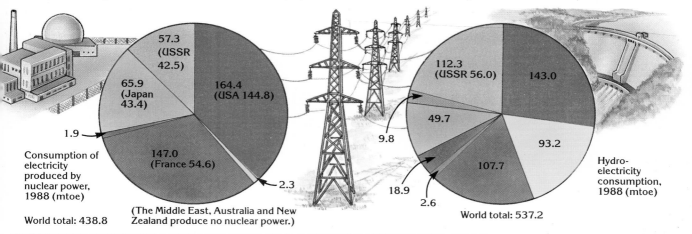

57.3 (USSR 42.5)
65.9 (Japan 43.4)
164.4 (USA 144.8)
1.9
147.0 (France 54.6)
2.3

Consumption of electricity produced by nuclear power, 1988 (mtoe)

World total: 438.8

(The Middle East, Australia and New Zealand produce no nuclear power.)

112.3 (USSR 56.0)
143.0
49.7
9.8
93.2
107.7
18.9
2.6

Hydro-electricity consumption, 1988 (mtoe)

World total: 537.2

Primary energy figures

If, for each area, you add together the consumption figures for the five energy sources, you arrive at a "primary energy" consumption figure (in mtoe) for each area. Each of these charts breaks down this total (1988) figure (given below each chart) to show the percentages of the different sources consumed.

Key
- Oil
- Natural gas
- Coal
- Nuclear
- Hydro

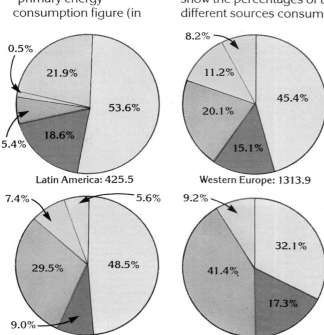

Latin America: 425.5
0.5%
21.9%
53.6%
18.6%
5.4%

Western Europe: 1313.9
8.2%
11.2%
45.4%
20.1%
15.1%

Middle East: 194.9
1.3% 1.3%
27.9%
69.5%

North America: 2192.4 (USA 1940.8)
6.5%
7.5%
39.4%
23.5%
23.1%

Asia: 884.7 (Japan 399.9)
7.4% 5.6%
29.5%
48.5%
9.0%

Australia and New Zealand: 106.9 (Australia 90.8)
9.2%
41.4%
32.1%
17.3%

Socialist countries: 2745.2 (USSR 1396.6)
2.1% 4.1%
24.2%
45.4%
24.2%

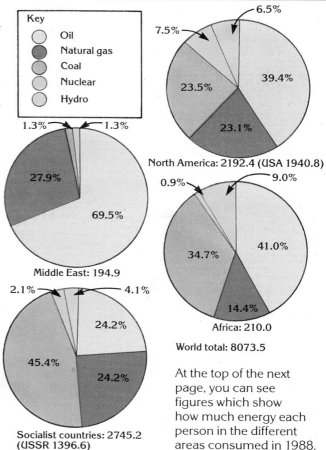

Africa: 210.0
0.9% 9.0%
41.0%
34.7%
14.4%

World total: 8073.5

At the top of the next page, you can see figures which show how much energy each person in the different areas consumed in 1988.

41

Energy use and population

This graph looks at the 1988 primary energy consumption figures, shown on page 41, in terms of how much energy (on average) was used per person in each of the areas. The figures are worked out by dividing the total primary energy consumption of each area by its population.

It must be remembered that the primary energy figures are based on the five "major" energy sources, and that other sources of energy, such as wood, animal waste and refuse, and also solar, wind and wave power, are not taken into account.

The area groups are the same as on pages 40-41 (for example, "Asia" still means non-communist Asia), but some countries have been separated out. You can see that there are some very large differences between the rich and poor areas of the world. One person in North America, for example, used over 23½ times more energy than a person in Africa.

Tonnes of oil or equivalent (see pages 40 and 41) used per head in 1988

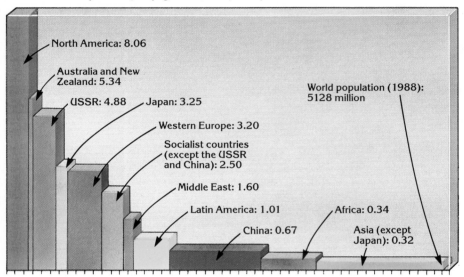

Population (millions). Each notched section represents 100 million.

Many of the countries which produce and use only a small amount of energy at the moment want to improve their living standards, but this would mean that they would greatly increase their energy use.

As you can see from the graph on the left, there were far more people using a small amount of energy in 1988 than there were using large amounts. If they all increased their energy use, the drain on the world's reserves would be enormous (and so would the increase in environmental damage). Below and at the top of page 43, there are some maps which show the state of the world's energy reserves.

World fossil fuel reserves

These special maps are based on the area groups on pages 40-41 (though in two cases, Australia and New Zealand are put together with Asia, because their figures are too small to single them out individually).

Most of the areas are in roughly the right geographical position, but their sizes are not their geographical sizes. The number of little squares each area occupies shows the known reserves of oil, gas and coal in that area in 1988. You can see how the Middle East dominates the oil map, the Middle East and the USSR dominate the gas map, and the USA, the USSR and China dominate the coal map.

Key to country groups

- North America
- Latin America
- Western Europe
- Middle East
- Africa
- Asia
- Australia and New Zealand
- Asia, Australia and New Zealand
- Socialist countries

Known oil reserves in billion barrels (1 square = 1 billion barrels)

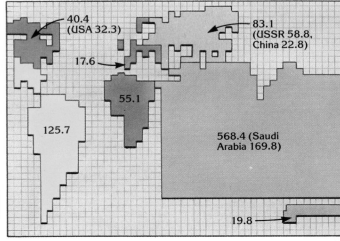

Known natural gas reserves in trillion cubic metres (1 square = 0.1 trillion cubic metres)

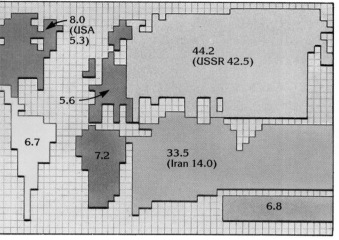

8.0 (USA 5.3)
44.2 (USSR 42.5)
5.6
6.7
7.2
33.5 (Iran 14.0)
6.8

Known coal reserves in billion tonnes (1 square = 1 billion tonnes)

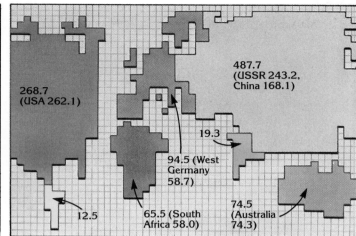

487.7 (USSR 243.2, China 168.1)
268.7 (USA 262.1)
19.3
94.5 (West Germany 58.7)
12.5
65.5 (South Africa 58.0)
74.5 (Australia 74.3)

The graphs below show how long the reserves of each area would last, if they continued to be produced (brought out of the ground) at the same (average) rate as that area produced them in 1988 (see page 40). The figure for the whole world shows how long world reserves would last if we continued to produce oil, coal and gas at the average 1988 rate (the average of the rates of all the countries).

The danger is that we will continue to increase our demand for energy and, because of this, our rates of production. This would mean that the reserves would not even last as long as these graphs show.

Years of oil reserves remaining

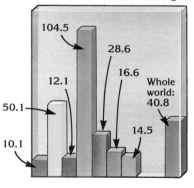

104.5
28.6
12.1
16.6
Whole world: 40.8
50.1
14.5
10.1

Years of gas reserves remaining

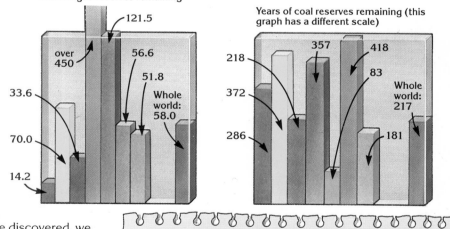

121.5
over 450
56.6
51.8
33.6
Whole world: 58.0
70.0
14.2

Years of coal reserves remaining (this graph has a different scale)

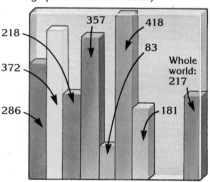

357
418
218
83
372
Whole world: 217
286
181

Although more oil, gas or coal may be discovered, we cannot rely on this. We must become much more energy efficient (use less energy in future years), so we can make the reserves last longer. In particular, the countries which use the most energy per head at the moment (see page 42) must drastically reduce their energy use, and help the poor countries build up their industries in the most energy-efficient way.

Another way we can secure enough energy in the future is to develop our use of renewable sources, such as the sun and the wind. This will also help to reduce the environmental damage caused by burning fossil fuels.

Notes on units and numbers used on these pages

1. One tonne (metric ton) = 1,000 kilograms or 0.98 tons (imperial tons).

2. One barrel = 0.136 tonnes or 42 US gallons (35 imperial gallons).

3. One billion = one thousand million (1,000,000,000) and one trillion = one million million (1,000,000,000,000). These are USA values (in some countries, such as the UK, a billion is one million million, and a trillion is one million million million).

The economics of energy

There are many costs and benefits involved in the production of energy. Large amounts of money are spent when a power station is built, and also to keep it working. If the power station has been planned properly, though, this expenditure should be balanced, and overtaken, by the amount of money earned from selling the energy, and from other sideline benefits.

There are also hidden costs and benefits involved in producing energy, and these may be difficult to measure in terms of money. People are now becoming more aware of such things as pollution and noise disturbance, and it is important that these factors are also considered. Below you can see these factors included in an economic plan of a refuse-burning power station (see pages 28-29).

Energy is produced in a refuse-burning power station by burning household and commercial refuse (waste). This would otherwise simply be buried in large tips, called landfill sites. An ideal, energy-efficient, refuse-burning power station would also be part of a CHP system (see page 34), so that the hot water it produces is not wasted.

Other costs (not normally considered)

Damage to the environment due to the release of gases (such as hydrogen chloride, carbon dioxide and sulphur dioxide), dust and particles of heavy metals (such as mercury and cadmium).

Disturbance to the local community, due to such things as noise, smells, soot and extra traffic.

Benefits (normally considered)

Money from selling electricity

Money from the local authority as a payment for taking away its refuse.

Money from selling metals and other materials extracted from the refuse.

Money from selling hot water (produced in the power station) as part of a CHP system (see page 36).

Costs (normally considered)

Paying the fees and wages of the architects, engineers and construction workers who designed and built the power station, and the management and workers who operate it.

Buying the land the power station is built on and the materials to build it with.

Buying basic supplies and paying for repairs and new machine parts needed to keep the power station running.

Paying for transport to bring the refuse and other supplies to the power station, and take away the ash.

Other costs, such as insurance, rates and possibly interest payments (extra payments that must be made if money was borrowed to help start up the power station).

Other benefits (not normally considered)

The amount of refuse to be buried is reduced to a relatively small amount of ash. This means the landfill site(s) will last longer and transport costs are lower because fewer lorries are needed.

There is less danger of pollution caused by poisonous substances seeping into local water from the landfill site(s).

Up to now, the other, "extra" costs have almost always been ignored during planning, because they are difficult to assess. It is also particularly true of power stations burning fossil fuels that pollution is very much accepted as a fact, and is not seen as a cost. So, from this point of view, there are not really any other "extra" benefits which can be gained from operating in a different way.

To work out the economics of a truly "environment-friendly" power station, the extra costs should be included, as far as possible, in the figures. For example, the release of harmful substances could be greatly reduced by spending more money on anti-pollution devices. So the price of these devices should be put in the "costs" column. It is very important that people begin to plan in this way, so that the true cost of producing energy can be calculated.

Further information

Below are some addresses of organizations, groups and government offices which are concerned with energy resources and the production, consumption and conservation of energy. They will be able to provide you with further information.

If you want to find out about smaller, local groups that are concerned with energy issues, you could try asking at your local library or writing to the main offices of the organizations listed below, to see if they have local branches.

International

International Energy Agency,
2, Rue Andre-Pascal,
75775 Paris Cedex 16, France

International Atomic Energy
Authority,
Wagramerstrasse 5,
P.O. Box 100,
A-1400 Vienna, Austria

Friends of the Earth International,
26-28 Underwood Street,
London N1 7JQ, England

Greenpeace International,
Keizersgracht 176,
1016 DW, Amsterdam
The Netherlands

United Kingdom

National Power,
Sudbury House,
15 Newgate Street,
London EC1A 7AU

Powergen,
53 New Broad Street,
London EC2M 1JJ

Energy Efficiency Office,
1 Palace Street,
London SW1E 5HE

Association for the Conservation of
Energy,
9 Sherlock Mews,
London W1M 3RH

UK Atomic Energy Authority,
11 King Charles II Street,
London SW1Y 4QP

National Centre for Alternative
Technology,
Machynlleth,
Powys SY20 9AZ

United States of America

American Council for an Energy
Efficient Economy,
1001 Connecticut Avenue NW,
Washington DC 20036

Electric Power Research Institute,
3412 Hillview Avenue,
P.O. Box 10412,
Palo Alto,
California 94303

Solar Energy Research Institute,
1617 Cole Boulevard,
Golden,
Colorado 80401

World Resources Institute,
1735 New York Avenue NW,
Washington DC 20006

World Watch Institute,
1776 Massachusetts Avenue NW,
Washington DC 20036

Environmental Defense Fund,
257 Park Avenue South,
New York 10010

Australia and New Zealand

Energy Information Centre,
139 Flinders Street,
Melbourne 3000,
Victoria

Energy Planning Office,
Energy Information Centre,
222 North Terrace,
Adelaide 5000,
South Australia

State Energy Commission,
465 Wellington Street,
Perth 6000,
Western Australia

Canada

Atomic Energy of Canada,
344 Slater Street,
Ottawa,
Ontario K1A 0S4

Energy Resources Conservation
Board,
640-5 Avenue S.W.
Calgary,
Alberta T2P 3G4

Energy Probe Research Foundation,
100 College Street,
Toronto,
Ontario M5G 1L5

Department of Energy, Mines and
Resources,
580 Booth Street,
Ottawa,
Ontario K1A 0E4

Ontario Hydro,
700 University Avenue,
Toronto,
Ontario M5G 1X6

Australian Conservation Federation,
672B Glenferrie Road,
Hawthorn 3122,
Victoria

Victorian Solar Energy Council,
10th Floor,
270 Flinders Street,
Melbourne 3000,
Victoria

Ministry of Energy,
P.O. Box 2337,
Wellington,
New Zealand

Glossary

Atoms. The "building blocks" of all substances. They are very tiny particles, each one made up of even tinier particles called **protons**, **neutrons** and **electrons**. The different amounts of these determine what substance the atom is.

Biogas. Gas produced by rotting material such as animal manure and other farm, household and industrial waste. The gas contains **methane** and can be used as a fuel to heat buildings or generate electricity.

Biomass. All types of organic (animal or plant) material. Biomass is a store of energy, which can be converted into other types of energy, e.g. wood, straw or animal dung can be burnt to produce heat and light energy.

Chemical energy. Energy stored in a substance and released during a chemical reaction. Fuels such as wood, coal, oil and food all contain chemical energy. The reaction when they are burnt (or digested) releases the energy, e.g. as heat and light energy.

Conductor. A material through which heat or an electric current can flow easily. Copper and iron are both good conductors.

Conservation of energy. When energy changes from one form to another (e.g. when fuel burns), the total amount of energy before the change is always the same as the total amount of energy after the change. The energy is always conserved. It cannot be destroyed.

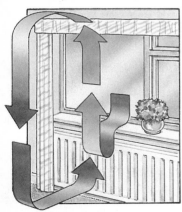

Convection. One way that heat travels through a liquid or gas. When heated, the **molecules** near the heat source gain more energy, moving faster and further apart. The heated liquid or gas then moves upwards, because it is now less dense and lighter. Cooler liquid or gas, with more densely-packed molecules, sinks to take its place.

Distillation. The process of separating a mixture of liquids by heating. The different liquids evaporate at different temperatures, the one with the lowest boiling point evaporating first. The separated gases are condensed back into liquids by cooling.

Dynamo. A machine which changes **kinetic energy** into electrical energy.

Electromagnetic energy. Energy which travels in waves, such as ultra-violet radiation. It can be thought of as a combination of electric and magnetic energy.

Electromagnetism. The effect whereby a magnetic field is produced around a wire when an electric current is passed through the wire. Electromagnets (see pages 23 and 24) use this principle.

Electromotive force. The force needed to drive an electric current in an electric circuit. It is measured in volts.

Electrons. Particles which form part of an **atom**. They move around its **nucleus**.

Fission. The splitting up of the **nucleus** of a heavy **atom** into two (or more) lighter nuclei. It releases huge amounts of energy.

Fossil fuels. Fuels which result from the compression of the remains of living matter over millions of years. Coal, oil and natural gas are all fossil fuels.

Friction. The resistance between two touching surfaces (or one surface and the air) when they move over each other. This slows down the moving object(s). Some of the kinetic energy changes into other types of energy.

Fusion. The joining together (fusing) of the **nuclei** of two or more **atoms** into one heavier nucleus. It releases vast amounts of energy.

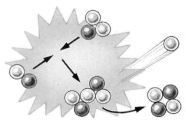

Generator. A device which turns **mechanical energy** into electricity. The mechanical energy may be provided by an engine or a **turbine**.

Geothermal energy. The heat energy which is produced by natural processes inside the Earth. It can be extracted from hot springs, reservoirs of hot water deep below the ground or by breaking open the rock itself.

Greenhouse effect. The warming effect produced when radiation cannot escape to the atmosphere or space. A good example is what happens in a greenhouse (hence the name). Short-wave radiation from the sun penetrates the glass of the greenhouse, and is absorbed by the plants, but the long-wave radiation that the plants emit cannot get back out through the glass. Carbon dioxide and other gases in the atmosphere act like the greenhouse glass. The levels of these gases are increasing, so the climate is slowly getting warmer (called global warming).

Grid system. A network of cables which carry electricity from power stations, where it is produced, to the cities, towns and villages of a country.

Hydrocarbons. Chemical compounds which contain only carbon and hydrogen **atoms**. They are the dominant compounds in **fossil fuels**.

Hydro-electricity. Electricity which is produced from moving water. In a typical hydro-electric power station, the water turns **turbines**, which are attached to **generators**.

Insulator. A bad **conductor**, e.g. wood or plastic. These substances slow down the progress of electricity or heat energy.

Joule (J). The unit of measurement of energy. One thousand joules equals one kilojoule (kJ). Kilojoules are normally used in measurements, since measured quantities are usually at least a thousand joules.

Kinetic energy. The energy of movement. The faster an object moves, the more kinetic energy it has. Also, the more mass a moving object has, the more kinetic energy it has.

Methane. A gas (a **hydrocarbon**) which is produced by organic (plant and animal) matter when it rots in the absence of oxygen. Natural gas is mainly methane.

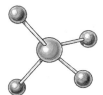

Molecules. Particles which normally consist of two or more **atoms** joined together, e.g. a water molecule is made up of two hydrogen atoms and one oxygen atom.

Neutrons. Particles which form part of the **nucleus** of an atom (**protons** make up the rest of the nucleus).

Nucleus (pl. nuclei). The central part of an **atom**, made up of tightly-packed **protons** and **neutrons**.

Photosynthesis. The process by which green plants make food (carbohydrates) from water and carbon dioxide, using the energy in sunlight. The food is a store of **chemical energy** inside the plants.

Photovoltaic cell. Another name for a **solar cell**.

Potential energy. Energy that is stored in an object due to its being within the influence of a force field, e.g. a magnetic or gravitational field.

Power. The rate at which energy is produced or used. It is generally stated as the rate of doing work or the rate of change of energy. Power is measured in watts (W). One watt equals one **joule** per second.

Protons. Particles which form part of the **nucleus** of an atom. The other particles in the nucleus are **neutrons**.

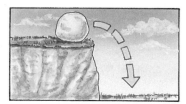

Radioactivity. A property of the **atoms** of certain substances, due to the fact that their **nuclei** are unstable. They give out energy in the form of particles or waves.

Reactor. Part of a nuclear power station – the structure inside which **fission** occurs in millions of atomic **nuclei**, producing vast amounts of heat energy.

Renewable energy. Energy from sources which are constantly available in the natural world, such as wind, water or the sun.

Solar cell. A device, usually made from silicon, which converts some of the energy in sunlight directly into electricity.

Turbine. A device with blades, which is turned by a force, e.g. that of wind, water or high pressure steam. The **kinetic energy** of the spinning turbine is converted into electricity in a **generator**.

Index

We are grateful to "Green Teacher",
Machynlleth, Powys, Wales, for
permission to use adaptations of
material previously published by
themselves (projects on pages 25, 27, 30
and 33).

The figures on pages 40-43 are based on
those given in the BP Statistical Review of
World Energy (July 1989), produced by
The British Petroleum Company plc,
Britannic House, Moor Lane, London
EC2Y 9BU, England, and the World
Population Data Sheet, produced by
Population Concern, 231 Tottenham
Court Road, London W1P 9AE, England.
We are grateful for permission to use
these statistics.